Salads

the art of creating cool food

TAMARA MILSTEIN

R&R PUBLICATIONS MARKETING PTY LTD

MAJOR CREDITS
Published by:
R&R Publications Marketing Pty Ltd
(ACN 083 612 579)
PO Box 254
Carlton North, Victoria 3054 Australia
Australia-wide Toll Free: 1 800 063 296

© Richard Carroll
Publisher: Richard Carroll
Author: Tamara Milstein
Food Photography: Andrew Elton
Food Stylist: Stephanie Souvlis
Assistant Home Economists: Jenny Fanshaw, Julie Ballard
Cover Design: Carlton Studios
Creative Director: Paul Sims
Layout: Jenny Ring
Editor/Proofreader: Jenny Ring

The National Library of Australia
Cataloguing-in-Publication Data
Milstein, Tamara, 1965–.
  Salad
  Includes index.
  ISBN 1 740220 13 7
  1. Salad. I. Title
641.83

This Edition printed October 1999
Computer typeset in Optima and Monotype Script Bold by:
R&R Publications Marketing Pty Ltd, Brunswick, Victoria Australia
Film Scanning: PICA Overseas, Singapore
Printed by: APP, Singapore

The Publishers would like to acknowledge and thank the following contributors for their support and assistance with the provision of materials for photography and food for photography and recipe development:
Villeroy & Boch, Brookvale, NSW, Australia
Accoutrement, Mosman and Woollahra, NSW, Australia
Baytree Kitchen Shop, Woollahra, NSW, Australia
Olson & Blake, Australia
Photography credits: Keith Platt pages 6, 22, 34 & 74

Contents

Introduction

Salad . . . such a simple word, which these days conjures up a never-ending selection of exciting and stimulating flavours!

Just a few years ago, 'salad' implied a bowl of healthy but mundane ingredients such as lettuce, tomato and cucumber, and in those days a salad was just a side dish. But, oh, how things have changed.

I love to whip up a bowl full of crunchy vegetables garnished with a little something extra that adds texture and flavour such as toasted nuts, crispy fried shallots or coconut shavings, and the contents of my refrigerator are all the inspiration I need.

With salads today, anything goes!

You can base them on purchased cooked Asian noodles and add some bok choy, sliced water chestnuts, Asian sauces and perhaps some ginger. You may be inspired by some leftover rice and add some Indian spices, chickpeas, roasted garlic and spinach or perhaps you have some leftover roast lamb or chicken. Add some spinach leaves, toasted pine nuts and a drizzle of balsamic vinegar and you have a feast fit for a king.

The only rule you must follow when creating salads from the recipes in this book, or when inventing your own, is that the produce must be of the highest quality. Fresh vegetables should be crisp and firm with no sign of soft spots or spoilage, and it is crucial that these are purchased and stored correctly.

Tender leaf vegetables such as rocket, spinach and bok choy should be purchased within two or three days of use and should be washed and dried well, then stored in a plastic bag in the vegetable section of your refrigerator.

More hardy vegetables like pumpkin, capsicum, carrots and onions can survive happily in the crisper for several days.

Herbs should also be washed and dried thoroughly before use, stored in a plastic bag in the refrigerator and used within two days. Of course, if you have your own herb garden or pots of herbs just pick them before use and wash and dry well.

If you are planning to make a salad a day or two before serving, unless specified in the recipe all salads should remain 'undressed' and stored in the refrigerator covered with plastic wrap.

In most cases, the dressing can be made up to two days ahead and stored in the refrigerator. To use, bring the dressing back to room temperature then whisk or mix again before tossing through the salad before serving.

Salads containing meat, chicken or fish must be consumed within two days but salads based on potato, rice or pasta can often survive well for several days stored in the refrigerator.

While some of the recipes in this book indicate the number of serves, others do not as the salad is suitable as a main dish or accompaniment. As a general rule, each recipe makes enough to fill a large salad bowl. Note that entrée refers to the first part of a meal, before the main course, rather than the American entrée which is a main course.

Above all, realise the flexibility and versatility of salads and take them from their position as an unappreciated side dish to the starring role of an entrée, main course, picnic dish or buffet choice.

Asian Flavours

These days, Asian cooking is so much a part of our culinary repertoire. The days when Chinese was the only Asian style we were familiar with are long gone and today we are far more likely to create dishes with the flavours of Vietnam, Malaysia or Thailand.

Many of us are on very familiar terms with fish sauce, coconut milk and lemongrass while those who are really inspired have begun to plant our gardens with kaffir lime trees, pots of coriander, Thai basil and Vietnamese mint so that we have quality Asian ingredients whenever we need them.

There are endless selections of Asian noodles in Asian food stores and different grains of rice to experiment with.

Supermarkets are lining their shelves with a myriad of Asian sauces and condiments. Nam pla, hoisin, and teriyaki sauces vie for our attention while rows of brightly coloured jars of chillies and pastes are just waiting for our tastebuds to be piqued.

While the recipes within this chapter will gently lead the novice to cook with confidence, the delicious flavour combinations will inspire those with more experience in Asian ingredients.

Malaysian Avocado Rice Salad

Rice is such an important part of the Malaysian diet. It is served at every meal in many varied and unusual ways. The recipe for this light and refreshing herbal rice salad was given to me by a close friend who has spent many years working in Kuala Lumpur.

Serves 8

Ingredients

Rice:
5cm (2") piece turmeric, peeled
5cm (2") piece galangal, peeled
2 small red chillies, seeded and minced
8 kaffir lime leaves
6 cups cooked jasmine rice
½ cup toasted, shredded coconut
30 leaves of Thai basil
30 leaves of Vietnamese mint
3 tablespoons fish sauce

2 tablespoons black sesame seeds

Dressing:
¾ cup olive oil (light)
⅓ cup lime juice
¼ cup lemon juice
½ cup Thai basil leaves
10 sprigs coriander, leaves and stem
2 cloves garlic, minced
1 small red chilli, minced
1 avocado, peeled
1 tablespoon palm sugar

Method

Very finely julienne the turmeric, galangal, chilli and kaffir lime leaves and mix with the rice. Add the toasted coconut, basil and mint and mix in the fish sauce. Set aside.

Make the dressing: purée all dressing ingredients in a food processor until thick, smooth and creamy and fold through the rice.

Arrange on a platter and serve at room temperature, sprinkled with the black sesame seeds.

Variation: Try adding some cooked fish to this salad for a lovely summer lunch. Bake or grill a piece of salmon then flake into small pieces. Mix with the rice and other ingredients and serve.

Asian Chicken Bok Choy Salad

(photographed on page 7)

If you are looking for a main course salad, this may be the perfect choice. This is an interesting salad, full of textures and flavours—substantial enough for a hearty appetite without weighing you down. Although not traditional, the yoghurt gives the dressing enough body to coat the ingredients beautifully.

Serves 6-8

Ingredients

8 fresh or dried shiitake mushrooms*
10g (1/3 oz) black cloud fungus*

4 cups shredded cooked chicken, skin off
(about 800g/28oz)
2 x 500g (1lb) packets fresh Asian Hokkien noodles
200g (7oz) fresh snow peas, diagonally sliced
4 baby bok choy, well washed and leaves separated
1 diced red capsicum
4 spring onions, finely sliced
250g (8oz) can sliced water chestnuts, drained

1 tablespoon freshly minced ginger
1/4 cup plain low-fat yoghurt
3 tablespoons kecap manis (Indonesian sweet soy)
1 tablespoon hoisin sauce (Chinese barbecue sauce)
3 tablespoons mirin (sweet Japanese rice wine)
3 tablespoons rice vinegar
3 tablespoons sweet chilli sauce
1 tablespoon fish sauce
juice of 1 lime
salt and pepper to taste

2 tablespoons slivered almonds, toasted
1 bunch of chervil (or parsley or coriander)

Method

If using dried shiitake, soak in hot water for 15 minutes then drain and slice. If using fresh shiitake, slice finely. Soak the black cloud fungus for 15 minutes then drain. Rinse the soaked mushrooms thoroughly in cold water.

Place the shredded cooked chicken in a large bowl. Break up the cooked noodles under hot running water until the noodles have separated then shake off excess water and add to the chicken. Add the mushrooms, sliced snow peas, well washed baby bok choy leaves, diced capsicum, sliced spring onions and water chestnuts and toss well.

In a jug, whisk together the ginger, yoghurt, kecap manis, hoisin, mirin, rice vinegar, sweet chilli, fish sauce, lime juice and salt and pepper to taste. Add to the chicken salad and toss very well until all the ingredients are coated. Garnish with the toasted slivered almonds and chopped chervil and serve.

*Available from Asian supermarkets and food stores.

Caramelized Ocean Trout Salad with Cellophane Noodles

After a delicious dinner in Phuket I created this light and easy dish which is low in fat and high in flavour.

Ingredients

2 tablespoons olive oil
10 shallots, chopped
1 cup palm sugar*

100ml (3½ oz) fish sauce*
½ cup fresh ginger, julienned
10 small chillies, halved, seeds removed and julienned**
2 tablespoons lime juice

200g (7oz) cellophane noodles
1 bunch fresh coriander leaves, chopped

500g (17oz) ocean trout fillets,
cut into 3cm-thick (1¼") strips
chillies and coriander leaves, extra, for garnish

Method

Heat the olive oil and gently sauté the chopped shallots until golden. Add the palm sugar and heat in the pan until the sugar has dissolved. Cook on a medium heat until the mixture has caramelized, about 5 minutes, stir well. Add the fish sauce, ginger, chillies and lime juice and stir well until combined. Keep hot.

Soak the cellophane noodles in hot water until they have softened, about 10 minutes, then refresh in cold water. Drain then add the coriander leaves and just enough palm sugar sauce to moisten the noodles.

Meanwhile, pan fry or grill the fish fillets until just cooked.

Arrange the noodles on individual plates then place the fish pieces decoratively on the cellophane noodles. Garnish with chillies and extra coriander leaves and spoon more sauce over.

*Available from Asian grocery stores.
**If you want the dish to be extra hot, then simple halve the chillies and leave the seeds inside.

Gingered Almond Broccoli Salad with Cellophane Noodles

I love the combination of spicy fresh ginger and chewy cellophane noodles, and in this recipe the texture of broccoli and the crunch of almonds completes the delicious picture.

Ingredients

Noodles:
100g (3½ oz) dried cellophane noodles
2 tablespoons fish sauce
2 tablespoons rice vinegar
2 tablespoons mirin (sweet Japanese rice wine)
1 teaspoon palm or brown sugar
½ cup chopped fresh coriander

Salad:
1 tablespoon peanut oil
1 tablespoon grated fresh ginger
1 very finely sliced small hot red chilli
4 cloves garlic, minced
4 spring onions, minced

500g (1lb) broccoli florets*, trimmed
10 fresh shiitake mushrooms, sliced
200g (7oz) baby corn
3 tablespoons soy sauce
3 tablespoons mirin, extra
2 tablespoons rice vinegar

1 cos lettuce, shredded
120g (4oz) blanched almonds, toasted
coriander, extra, for garnish

Method

First, prepare the noodles. Fill a deep jug or bowl with very warm water and soak the cellophane noodles for about 10 minutes or until they are soft and tender. Drain. Mix together the fish sauce, rice vinegar, 2 tablespoons of mirin and sugar then toss through the cellophane noodles. Add the coriander, mix well and set aside.

Heat the peanut oil in a wok and add the ginger, chilli, garlic and spring onions and toss thoroughly until the spring onions have wilted, about 3 minutes.

Add the broccoli florets and toss well until bright green. Add the mushrooms and corn and continue tossing over a high heat. Add the soy, 3 tablespoons of mirin and rice vinegar and continue cooking for 1 minute.

Add the noodles and mix well then remove the pan from the heat.

Divide the shredded lettuce amongst the plates then top with the broccoli noodle mixture. Garnish with toasted almonds and fresh, chopped coriander.

*When you buy heads of broccoli, trim each little head of broccoli from the main stem—this is called a floret.

Gingered Thai Rice Salad

This fabulously fragrant salad is refreshing and very easy to make. While there seems to be a lot of ingredients, the salad is actually very quick and easy to make. For a complete main course, I like to sear a thick fillet of white fish for each person, glazed in sweet chilli sauce and finished in the oven before it is perched on top of a mound of the rice salad.

Serves 6

Ingredients

2 cups long grain rice

5 spring onions, finely chopped on the diagonal
3 medium carrots, coarsely grated
4 baby bok choy, washed and chopped
2 kaffir lime leaves
½ cup coarsely chopped coriander
1½ cups chopped roasted peanuts
1 tablespoon black sesame seeds

2 tablespoons finely chopped Thai basil

Dressing: 2 tablespoons vegetable or peanut oil
juice of 2 limes (about 3 tablespoons)
3 tablespoons Thai fish sauce
2 tablespoons palm sugar
2 tablespoons sweet chilli sauce
1 tablespoon minced ginger
pinch of chilli powder or cayenne pepper
salt and pepper to taste

Method

First, cook the rice: bring a large pot of salted water to the boil then add the rice and simmer for 8-10 minutes or until tender. Drain and rinse thoroughly in cold water then drain again.

Meanwhile, make the dressing. Whisk together the oil, lime juice, fish sauce, palm sugar, sweet chilli sauce, ginger, chilli powder and salt and pepper and allow to sit until the rice is ready.

Prepare all the vegetables then mix thoroughly with the finely sliced lime leaves, coriander, chopped roasted peanuts and sesame seeds. Add the cooked rice and mix well.

Toss the rice and vegetable mixture with the dressing, tossing thoroughly to coat all the ingredients with the dressing then add the Thai basil and serve.

Shelley's Cabbage and Chinese Noodle Salad

My childhood friend Shelley brought this delightful salad to a barbecue recently, and I adored it's amalgam of flavours and interesting textures. Shelley was delighted to share the recipe with me, and although I have changed it a little (adding my favourite herb, coriander), this recipe is as easy to make and delicious to eat as the one she brought to that lovely barbecue!

Ingredients

Salad:
- ½ curly green cabbage
- 4 baby bok choy
- 8 spring onions
- ½ bunch fresh coriander

- ¾ cup flaked almonds, toasted
- ½ cup pine nuts, toasted

- 100g (3½ oz) fried Chinese noodles

Dressing:
- 4 tablespoons peanut oil
- 2 tablespoons balsamic vinegar
- 2 tablespoons fresh lime or lemon juice
- 1 tablespoon brown sugar (optional)
- 1 tablespoon soy sauce
- salt and cracked pepper to taste

Method

Finely shred the cabbage and transfer to a large mixing bowl. Thoroughly wash the bok choy then slice them widthways and add to the cabbage.

Wash the spring onions then slice finely on the diagonal, and add these to the cabbage mixture together with the washed and roughly chopped coriander.

Under the griller or in a dry frypan, toast the almonds and pine nuts and set aside to cool. Alternatively, toast the nuts in a microwave by spreading the nuts over the microwave plate and cooking them on HIGH for 2 minutes. Mix gently to distribute then cook for consecutive extra minutes until the nuts are as golden as you wish. Allow to cool.

Mix the nuts and noodles with the cabbage salad.

To make the dressing, whisk all the ingredients together with a whisk until thick. Drizzle over the salad and toss thoroughly then serve immediately.

Summer Greens with Lime and Coriander

A fabulous bright combination of vegetables with an extra tangy dressing of lime and coriander; equally delicious served hot or cold.

Serves 4-6

Ingredients

250g (8oz) snow peas, topped and tailed
2 bunches of asparagus, cut in half
250g (8oz) sugar snaps, topped and tailed

250g (8oz) fresh peas (shelled)
½ punnet cherry tomatoes, cut in half

Dressing:
2 tablespoons lime juice
3 tablespoons chopped coriander
½ cup olive oil
1 tablespoon white wine vinegar

Method

Blanch the snow peas, asparagus and sugar snaps in boiling water for 30 seconds, drain and refresh in a bowl of iced cold water. Drain well.

Cook peas in boiling water for 5 minutes, or until tender, drain and refresh in iced water. Drain well. Combine all vegetables and cherry tomatoes.

For the dressing whisk all ingredients until well combined and toss over vegetables and serve.

Vietnamese Green Papaya Salad

I love the freshness of green papaya. The flavour blends superbly with lime juice and really lends itself to the addition of other ingredients such as prawns, pork or chicken. The vegetables are easy to julienne using a v-slicer or mandoline.

Serves 8

Ingredients

Salad:
750g (26oz) approx. green papaya
4 spring onions, very finely julienned
half white radish, very finely julienned
12 leaves of Asian mint
12 leaves of Thai basil (or regular basil)
$\frac{1}{4}$ bunch coriander, leaves only
1 clove garlic, minced

2 tablespoons dried shrimp or crushed peanuts
extra Thai basil and Asian mint leaves, to garnish

Dressing:
$\frac{1}{4}$ teaspoon shrimp paste
2 tablespoons boiling water
3 tablespoons rice vinegar
3 tablespoons lime juice
2 tablespoons fish sauce
2 tablespoons sugar
1 tablespoon sweet chilli sauce

Method

Finely julienne the papaya and toss with the finely julienned spring onions, white radish, chopped fresh herbs and garlic.

To make the dressing, dilute the shrimp paste in 2 tablespoons boiling water, then whisk with all other dressing ingredients. If the sauce is a little too acidic, add a little extra water as required to dilute the flavour to your tastes. Continue whisking until the dressing is well mixed.

Toss the dressing through the papaya/vegetable mixture, taking care to disperse the dressing thoroughly.

Pile on a plate and sprinkle with peanuts or dried shrimp.

A Taste of Europe

The salads of Europe are as diverse as the countries that make up this exciting continent. While the very popular Mediterranean flavours are grouped in a chapter of their own, the less familiar flavours of continental Europe are showcased here.

Root vegetables have always been a necessary ingredient throughout the bitter cold of the Northern European winters and this has led to an exciting collection of recipes for the warmer months.

Experiment with a salad of roasted beetroot for a delicious introduction to the ways of the frugal European cook. Even the tender young leaves of the beetroot become part of the salad while crisp hazelnuts and sour cream complete this delicious recipe.

Potato salads are another European offering but, in traditional German style, these are bound with a piquant dressing of vinegar and lemon juice with fresh herbs rather than the heavy and fat-laden mayonnaise dressings favoured by American cooks.

There are other surprises here too, such as the timeless combination of apples, blue cheese and nuts served with witlof.

Warm Salad of Braised Leeks and Onions

This typically Germanic dish makes a fabulous accompaniment to an outdoor barbecue and is just as good when served with a herbed roast chicken. Make it a day ahead, if you have time, to intensify the flavours.

Ingredients

6 medium leeks
60ml (2oz) olive oil

1 cup chicken stock
½ cup white wine
6 small white onions
6 shallots
juice of a fresh lemon
2 teaspoons fresh thyme
2 teaspoons fresh marjoram
1 bay leaf
salt and freshly ground pepper

2 teaspoons balsamic vinegar

2 tablespoons finely chopped fresh parsley

Method

Trim the leeks to where the green meets the white and discard all the tough green stalks. Slice the remaining white parts into a julienne of thin pieces and swish through a bowl of cold water to remove any grit. Sauté in the olive oil.

Add the chicken stock, the wine, whole onions and shallots, lemon juice, thyme, marjoram, bay leaf and salt and pepper to taste. Bring to a simmer over medium heat and cook, uncovered, until tender, 20-25 minutes. Remove from the heat and let cool slightly. Stir in the balsamic vinegar.

Just before serving, remove the bay leaf. Place the leeks, onions, shallots and their marinade in a serving dish. Sprinkle with the parsley and serve.

Roasted Beetroot Salad with Balsamic and Dill

(photographed on page 23)

Fresh beetroot is one of life's culinary treasures. So many of us are used to the sugary sweetness of canned beetroot and never experience the mellow, earthy flavours of this vegetable when it is cooked and eaten immediately. Roasting brings out the sweetness and this marries magnificently with balsamic glaze. Fresh dill adds just a dash of colour.

Ingredients

24 very small beetroots, greens attached if possible
1 tablespoon olive oil

salt and freshly ground pepper to taste

1 tablespoon butter
2 tablespoons balsamic vinegar

3 tablespoons fresh dill, snipped
100g (3½ oz) hazelnuts, roasted and chopped
2 tablespoons sour cream or yoghurt (optional)
black pepper to taste

Method

If your beetroots have their greens attached, remove them and set aside. Wash the beetroots and scrub them until clean. Trim the bottom if necessary but be careful not to cut the beetroot itself.

Toss the beetroots and olive oil together then place them in a baking dish. Cover with foil or a lid and roast at 200°C (400°F) for 30-45 minutes or until tender.

Remove the beetroots from the oven and cool then peel the skin away and discard. Cut the beetroots in half lengthways and add salt and pepper to taste.

Meanwhile, wash the greens thoroughly to remove all traces of sand and grit. Heat the butter in a sauté pan and add the greens, tossing for 1 minute until wilted. Remove the greens and add the balsamic vinegar and bring to the boil, whisking with the butter. Return the peeled beetroots and toss them in the balsamic until it has reduced and leaves a shiny sheen on the beetroots.

Transfer the beetroots to a platter or bowl and arrange with the wilted beetroot leaves. Scatter over the dill and roasted hazelnuts, adding small dollops of the sour cream or yoghurt if desired. Add black pepper to taste.

Russian Cabbage Salad

Cabbage has been a staple ingredient in the Russian diet for centuries and over the years Russian housewives have become adept at creating interesting recipes out of this humble vegetable.

Ingredients

1kg (2lb) approx. crinkled cabbage

1 Spanish onion
6 spring onions
2 cloves garlic, minced
1/4 teaspoon chilli flakes
4 tablespoons fresh dill, chopped
4 tablespoons fresh parsley, chopped

100ml (3½ oz) olive oil
100ml (3½ oz) lemon or lime juice
1 tablespoon seed mustard
1 tablespoon honey

Method

Shred the cabbage as finely as possible and place in a mixing bowl.

In a separate bowl, add the chopped onion, sliced spring onions, garlic, chilli, dill and parsley and mix well, making sure that all the ingredients are thoroughly combined.

Whisk the olive oil, lemon or lime juice, mustard and honey together until well blended and pour over the cabbage together with the herb mixture.

Mix well and chill until ready to serve.

Spanish Carrot and Prawn Salad

This delicious salad is simple to make and is often served as a tapas or light appetizer with other small but flavoursome dishes, much like an Italian antipasto platter. Purchase large, cooked prawns with the shell and heads removed.

Serves 6

Ingredients

700g (1½ lb) carrots

4 cloves garlic
1 tablespoon fresh rosemary

60ml (2oz) virgin olive oil
1 teaspoon ground cumin
2 teaspoons mild paprika
40ml (1⅓ oz) white wine vinegar
salt and freshly ground pepper to taste

500g (1lb) large peeled, cooked prawns (tail on)
¼ cup chopped continental parsley

Method

Peel and trim the carrots then slice on the diagonal into 5mm slices. Bring a large pot of salted water to the boil and add the sliced carrots. Boil vigorously for 3-4 minutes or until almost crisp-tender then drain.

Meanwhile, peel the garlic and pound in a mortar and pestle with the fresh rosemary until the two are finely ground and fragrant. Alternatively, finely chop the garlic and rosemary together.

Heat a tablespoon of the oil in a small frypan and add the garlic and rosemary mixture, cumin and paprika and sauté for a minute or two until very fragrant. Remove from the heat and whisk in the remaining olive oil and white wine vinegar. Add salt and pepper to taste.

Toss the carrot slices and cooked prawns with the warm garlic rosemary dressing, making sure that all the ingredients are well coated. Garnish with fresh parsley.

Chill for at least 4 hours then serve cool or at room temperature. Serve with plenty of crusty bread if desired.

Warm Herbed Potato Salad

This potato salad is delicious served warm with roast meats as a substitute to oven-baked vegetables but is also very good cold, making it a good choice for a picnic lunch. Potato salads are popular in dozens of different varieties in Europe where cuisines are based around potatoes and other root vegetables.

Ingredients

1.5kg (3lb) Desiree or Pontiac potatoes

2 tablespoons olive oil
4 white onions, peeled and sliced

$\frac{1}{4}$ cup chopped fresh dill
$\frac{1}{4}$ cup chopped fresh chervil
$\frac{1}{4}$ cup chopped fresh parsley
zest of 1 lemon
salt and freshly ground pepper to taste

Dressing: $\frac{2}{3}$ cup olive oil
3 tablespoons white wine vinegar
juice of 1 lemon
3 cloves garlic

Method

Cut unpeeled (well washed) potatoes into large chunks and boil in salted water for 10 minutes or until tender but not soft.

In a separate pan, heat the olive oil and sauté the onions over high heat until golden, about 8 minutes. Turn down the heat, cover and cook slowly for 20 minutes.

Drain potatoes and return to the saucepan. In a jug, whisk the olive oil, white wine vinegar, lemon juice and garlic until thickened. Pour over the hot potatoes and toss, adding all the fresh herbs and lemon zest with salt and lots of freshly ground pepper to taste.

Add the caramelised onions and toss thoroughly.

Witlof Salad with Apples, Blue Cheese and Pecans

For lovers of blue cheese, this salad is close to perfection. For those who don't find blue cheese appealing, simply substitute brie, camembert or fresh goats cheese. Serve this salad on the day it is made for best results. As this salad is popular in Germany in summer, a chilled white wine and some crusty bread as accompaniments make this a wonderful light meal.

Serves 6

Ingredients

5 heads witlof (Belgian endive)

1 Red Delicious apple, cored, quartered, thinly sliced
1 Granny Smith apple

200g (7oz) young rocket leaves

1 cup coarsely chopped pecans, toasted
100g (3½ oz) crumbled blue cheese such as Gorgonzola or Blue Castello

¼ cup olive oil
¼ cup walnut oil
¼ cup sherry wine vinegar
1 large shallot, minced
salt and pepper to taste

Method

Cut the witlof in half, lengthwise then lay the witlof cut side down on a board and cut the leaves into thin strips.

Thinly slice the unpeeled apples and toss with the lemon juice.

Wash the rocket leaves and drain well.

Combine witlof strips, apple slices, rocket, toasted pecans and blue cheese in a large bowl.

Whisk the oils, vinegar and shallot in small bowl then season to taste with salt and pepper.

Drizzle the dressing over the salad and toss thoroughly. Serve immediately.

Middle Eastern Accents

A wander through an ancient market in any Middle Eastern city will inspire you to create salads flavoured with fresh mint, ground cumin and copious quantities of garlic and black pepper.

*W*hile many salads such as tabbouleh are popular in several Middle Eastern countries, each region stamps the salad with a flavour and style all its own. For example, Turkish tabbouleh is flavoured with a piquant red pepper condiment that colours the grain while adding a complex flavour.

*C*ouscous is a very popular ingredient throughout the Middle East and is one of the simplest ingredients to use. Flavour it simply with crushed nuts and fresh chopped herbs for a deliciously simple salad or side dish.

*A*dding small quantities of meat, chicken or seafood to Middle Eastern vegetable and grain salads adds flavour and interest without making them too heavy.

*D*ried spices are used subtly to add flavour and dried herbs are also popular. Remember that dried herbs and spices lose their flavour quickly so should be purchased in small quantities. Store them well wrapped in the freezer and they will taste fresh for months.

Smoked Eggplant Salad

Eggplants are a staple vegetable throughout the Middle East and they are used in dozens of soups, spreads, baked vegetable dishes and more. More like a dip than a salad, this is one of the simplest and most delicious recipes and keeps well in the refrigerator for up to a week.

Ingredients

6 large purple eggplants

6-8 garlic cloves
salt to taste
juice of 1-2 lemons
2 tablespoons yoghurt or mayonnaise

2 tablespoons chopped parsley or coriander
1 teaspoon chopped fresh mint (optional)

Method

Heat a barbecue until coals are red hot then place the eggplants directly on the barbecue plate and allow them to char all over turning often, about 30-40 minutes until they look like deflated purple balloons and the skin is blackened. (If you don't have a barbecue, you can do this in a grill pan or old frypan set over a gas stove).

When the eggplants have cooled, cut them in half and scrape out all the flesh into a bowl, discarding the skin.

Pound the garlic and salt together in a mortar and pestle until a paste forms then add this to the eggplant with the lemon juice and yoghurt or mayonnaise. Mix thoroughly then adjust seasoning with more salt and lemon juice if desired.

Arrange on a platter and sprinkle with parsley or coriander and a little fresh chopped mint.

Serve with pita bread.

Note: In many Turkish restaurants, the eggplant pulp is bleached by soaking in lemon and water after scraping the flesh from the skin. This is to make the pulp pale and creamy in colour but I find it an unnecessary step which takes away the rustic appearance of this wholesome recipe.

Armenian Stuffed Tomato Salad

(photographed on page 35)

I love the Arabic influence in this recipe. The nuts, dried fruits and spices are all typical of the Middle Eastern region where this recipe originates. Although these tomatoes were originally served warm, I served some at room temperature a few months ago on a bed of wilted spinach and the light, flavoursome meal was a great success!

Serves 8

Ingredients

8 large, round tomatoes

4 tablespoons olive oil
1 large onion, chopped finely
1 large leek, green part removed and finely chopped
3 cups steamed or boiled white or brown rice*
½ cup toasted pine nuts
¾ cup currants
½ cup parsley, chopped
1 tablespoon fresh mint, chopped
¾ teaspoon sea salt
½ teaspoon black pepper

2 cloves garlic, peeled and smashed
½ cup vegetable stock
½ cup white wine

500g (1lb) baby spinach leaves

Method

With a sharp knife, slice the tops off the tomatoes, and scoop out as much flesh as possible without damaging the exterior of the tomato. Chop the tomato pulp finely.

Heat the olive oil and cook the chopped onion and leek until slightly golden. Add the rice, tomato pulp, nuts, currants, parsley, mint, salt and pepper and sauté until the mixture is hot and well flavoured.

Fill each tomato with the rice mixture and replace the tops of the tomatoes. Combine the garlic, stock and white wine and drizzle around tomatoes.

Bake at 180°C (350°F) for 15 minutes.

Meanwhile, wash and dry the spinach leaves. When the tomatoes have finished cooking, remove them and toss the remaining hot liquid through the spinach, discarding the garlic.

Serve a mound of warm spinach on each plate with the tomato perched on top. Drizzle any remaining liquid over and serve.

*1 cup uncooked rice = 3 cups cooked rice.

Couscous Salad with Seafood and Fresh Mint

Refreshingly light, and with a lovely combination of flavours, this salad makes a great formal appetiser as well as a light lunch.

Serves 6

Ingredients

½ cup olive oil
60ml (2oz) fresh lemon juice
1 large garlic clove, minced
1 teaspoon celery seed
salt and pepper to taste

¼ teaspoon turmeric
¼ teaspoon cumin
400ml (13½ oz) boiling vegetable stock
500g (1lb) raw king prawns, peeled but tail on
200g (7oz) small calamari rings
300g (10½ oz) couscous

3 tomatoes, finely diced
2 stalks celery, finely sliced
6 spring onions, chopped
20 fresh mint leaves, finely sliced

Method

First, make the dressing. Whisk together the olive oil, lemon juice, garlic and celery seed until thick then season with salt and pepper. Set aside.

Add the turmeric and cumin to the simmering stock and stir. Add the prawns and calamari and poach gently for 2 minutes or until the prawns are orange then remove from the stock with a slotted spoon.

Place the couscous in a large bowl then pour the remaining spiced stock over. Stir well and cover then allow to stand until water is absorbed, about 10 minutes.

Fluff up with a fork then add the prawn and calamari mixture, diced tomatoes, celery, spring onions and some of the shredded mint leaves.

Add the dressing and mix well then garnish with mint leaves.

Israeli Cumquat Chicken Salad with Mixed Wild Rice

This piquant dish has all the flavour of Israeli citrus but the edge of the cumquat is reduced by adding some apricot and peach jam to the chicken marinade. This recipes makes a fabulous summer lunch and travels well for an outdoor picnic meal.

Serves 6-8

Ingredients

1kg (2lb) lean chicken, diced
1 teaspoon each of salt, pepper, paprika, ground cumin and onion powder
12-16 wooden/bamboo skewers

500ml (16½ oz) orange juice
¼ cup dry white wine
2 onions, diced
4 tablespoons apricot jam
4 tablespoons peach jam
4 tablespoons honey
2 tablespoons lemon juice
2 tablespoons lime juice
500g (1lb) fresh cumquats, or tinned if unavailable

¼ cup wild rice
½ cup brown rice
1 cup white rice

1 bunch basil, leaves thinly sliced
100g (3½ oz) toasted, chopped pistachio nuts

Method

Place the chicken cubes in a plastic bag and add the salt, pepper, paprika, ground cumin and onion powder and seal the bag. Shake vigorously to coat the chicken cubes with the spice mix then thread the spiced chicken pieces onto wooden skewers and place them in a shallow baking dish. Set aside.

Meanwhile mix the orange juice, wine, onions, both jams, honey, lemon and lime juice and cumquats and heat until just about to boil. Pour half this mixture (reserving the remaining mixture) over the chicken skewers and marinate for 2 hours.

While the chicken is marinating, prepare the rice. Bring a large pot of salted water to the boil and add the wild rice. Boil for 5 minutes then add the brown rice. Boil these together for a further 10 minutes before adding the white rice and simmering for 15 minutes. Drain thoroughly and keep warm.

Heat a grill pan, barbecue or griller and cook the chicken skewers until cooked through, brushing them with the remaining orange mixture as they cook.

To serve, fold the finely sliced fresh basil and chopped pistachio nuts through the rice then top with the chicken skewers, 2 per serve. Drizzle any remaining orange mixture over if desired.

Note: As an alternative serving suggestion, serve the chicken skewers and rice separately.

Middle Eastern Bean and Artichoke Salad

This salad is really an interesting combination of flavours from many different lands. We have herbs to maintain the African theme, chickpeas from the Middle East to add flavour and texture and an Italian inspired dressing with artichokes to carry the flavours. Like all the best salads, it keeps beautifully for several hours.

Ingredients

600g (21oz) green beans

2 x 400g (14oz) cans chickpeas
8 x preserved artichoke hearts, quartered
(either in brine or oil—your choice)
1 small Spanish onion, peeled and very finely sliced
1 medium carrot, grated
½ cup chopped parsley
½ cup chopped coriander
2 tablespoons fresh dill

2 tablespoons white wine vinegar
3 tablespoons olive oil
1 clove garlic, minced
1 teaspoon mustard
1 teaspoon ground cumin
juice of 1 large lemon
salt and pepper to taste

100g (3½ oz) hazelnuts, toasted and roughly chopped

Method

Steam, boil or microwave the beans until bright green and crisp-tender (do not overcook), drain well and refresh in cold water, then cut diagonally in half.

Place them in a large bowl and add the drained and rinsed chickpeas, quartered artichoke hearts, finely sliced Spanish onion, grated carrot, parsley, coriander and dill. Stir to combine thoroughly.

In a jug, whisk the vinegar, olive oil, garlic, mustard, cumin, lemon juice and salt and pepper. When emulsified (thick) pour over the vegetable mixture and toss very well to coat the vegetables in the dressing.

Sprinkle with toasted hazelnuts and serve.

Turkish Tabbouleh (Kisir)

Real Turkish tabbouleh is slightly more spicy than its other Middle Eastern cousins because it is bound with a hot red pepper paste. While this is available ready for purchase in Turkish spice shops, you can quite easily make your own. Of course, if you don't like spicy foods, you can omit it for a milder version.

Serves 8-10

Ingredients

1½ cups fine bulger (cracked wheat)

1 bunch spring onions, trimmed and finely sliced
2 large ripe tomatoes, seeded and diced
1 red capsicum, seeded and diced
1 small cucumber, peeled, seeded and diced
1 'packed' cup parsley, finely chopped
¼ cup fresh mint, sliced

⅓ cup red pepper paste (see below)
juice of 2 lemons
¼ cup olive oil
1 tablespoon pomegranate molasses
2 teaspoons ground cumin
salt and pepper to taste

Turkish red pepper paste (optional):
4 red capsicums, flesh only
4 hot red chillies
40ml (1⅓ oz) water
1 teaspoon salt
1 teaspoon sugar
20ml (⅔ oz) olive oil

Method

Cover the bulger with cool water and allow to stand for 30 minutes. Drain well, squeezing out any excess water. In a mixing bowl, combine the bulger, spring onions, tomatoes, capsicum, cucumber, parsley and mint and mix well. Add the red pepper paste (see below) and mix thoroughly until the salad takes on a lovely red hue.

Whisk together the lemon juice, olive oil, pomegranate molasses, cumin and salt and pepper. Pour the dressing over the vegetable mixture and toss thoroughly to make sure all the ingredients are coated. Add extra salt to taste if necessary then chill for 2 hours then serve cold or at room temperature.

Turkish red pepper paste: place the capsicums, chillies, water, salt, sugar and olive oil in a food processor and process until smooth. Transfer the mixture to a saucepan and simmer gently until the mixture is thick and the liquid has reduced, about 1 hour, stirring frequently. Cool.

The Mediterranean Salad Collection

The flavours of the Mediterranean hardly need an introduction. With accents of garlic, balsamic vinegar and basil, many of us have been creating salads with the flavours of the Mediterranean for years.

This chapter, however, offers a more extensive look at some of the cuisines that make up the Mediterranean basin. Inspiration from France comes in the form of a delicate duck salad flavoured with thyme and honey, or a fabulous French-inspired potato salad flavoured with the classic Roquefort cheese.

The traditional Greek flavours of olives and lemon shine in a pasta salad while other recipes showcase the lesser-known Italian regions.

Stock your pantry with quality olive oil and a selection of balsamic and wine vinegars and plant some seedlings of basil, thyme, marjoram and parsley and you will have most of the necessary ingredients at your fingertips!

Provençal Salad of Potatoes, Beans and Roquefort

The French use 'haricots verts' for this salad—slender green beans that are very young. If you cannot find those, use tender green beans that are as slim as possible. This salad travels very well and is a great salad to serve when you have large groups of people to feed.

Serves 6-8

Ingredients

2 tablespoons white wine vinegar
juice of 1 lemon
150ml (5oz) quality olive oil
1-2 tablespoons seeded mustard
salt and pepper to taste

1½ kg (3lb) small red potatoes, quartered
500g (1lb) slender green beans
180g (6½ oz) crumbled Roquefort cheese

½ cup walnuts, toasted and chopped
1 bunch of chives, coarsely snipped

Method

Preheat oven to 220°C (430°F).

First, make the vinaigrette. Whisk the vinegar, lemon juice, olive oil, mustard and salt and pepper until the vinaigrette is thick and emulsified.

Toss the quartered potatoes with 4 tablespoons of the vinaigrette until they are shiny and well coated. Transfer the potatoes to a baking dish and cook in the preheated oven for 40 minutes, or until tender and crisp around the edges.

Blanch the beans in salted boiling water until just tender, about 2 minutes, then immediately plunge into cold water to stop the cooking process. Toss with a little of the dressing while still warm.

To serve, toss the warm potatoes, green beans, crumbled cheese and a little extra dressing together in a large bowl until the mixture is well combined.

Arrange on a platter then scatter the toasted walnuts over the top. Sprinkle chives on top and serve.

Calabrian Salad

(photographed on page 47)

Salads such as this one are perfect summer accompaniments to meat, chicken or fish dishes but also make wonderful entrées. This dish is full of robust flavours and is even lovely as part of an antipasto platter.

Serves 6

Ingredients

4 fist-sized potatoes, scrubbed and washed, not peeled

8 firm Roma tomatoes

3 Spanish onions, peeled and sliced thinly,
then soaked in cold water for 30 minutes

15 small, whole, fresh basil leaves
1 heaped teaspoon dried oregano
4 tablespoons olive oil
3 tablespoons white or red wine vinegar
salt and pepper to taste

Method

Cover the potatoes in cold water and boil until just tender all the way through, about 15-20min. Drain and leave aside until just cool enough to handle, then peel and slice thinly.

Cut the tomatoes in half and remove the hard inner core. Slice the tomatoes and add them to the potatoes. Add the finely sliced Spanish onions and toss well.

Add the basil leaves, oregano, olive oil, vinegar and add a little salt and pepper. Toss everything carefully and serve at once.

Greek Orzo Salad with Olives and Capsicums

Refreshing and great with chargrilled lamb, this salad travels well and makes a great barbecue accompaniment.

Ingredients

350g (12oz) orzo or rice-shaped pasta

170g (6oz) feta cheese, crumbled
1 red capsicum, finely chopped
1 yellow capsicum, finely chopped
1 green capsicum, finely chopped
180g (6½ oz) pitted kalamata olives, chopped
4 spring onions, sliced
2 tablespoons drained capers

Dressing:
juice and zest of 2 lemons
1 tablespoon white wine vinegar
1 tablespoon minced garlic
1½ teaspoons dried oregano
1 teaspoon Dijon mustard
1 teaspoon ground cumin
100ml (3½ oz) olive oil

3 tablespoons pine nuts, toasted

Method

Cook the orzo in a large pot of boiling salted water until tender but still firm to bite. Drain and rinse with cold water then place in a large bowl with a little olive oil from the dressing ingredients.

Add the crumbled feta cheese, chopped capsicums, kalamata olives, spring onions and capers.

To make the dressing, whisk together the lemon juice and zest, vinegar, garlic, oregano, mustard and cumin in a small bowl. Gradually add the remaining olive oil then season to taste with salt and pepper.

Drizzle the dressing over the salad and toss thoroughly then garnish with the toasted pine nuts.

Roasted Beetroot, Orange and Fennel Salad

This lovely salad is brightly coloured and full flavoured with rich, earthy aromas. The slight rosemary accent adds depth and makes this a good accompaniment for lamb but is just as good with roast chicken.

Serves 6-8

Ingredients

5 large beetroots

1 tablespoon brown sugar
1 teaspoon salt
2 tablespoons chopped fresh rosemary
3 tablespoons olive oil

1 bulb fennel
3 blood oranges

150g (5oz) toasted hazelnuts, crushed

Dressing:
½ cup chopped dill
2 tablespoons balsamic vinegar
½ cup olive oil
salt and pepper to taste

Method

Heat the oven to 180°C (350°F).

Wash and trim the beetroots at root and stem ends but do not peel.

In a small bowl, mix together the brown sugar, salt, rosemary and the 3 tablespoons of olive oil until well blended then add the whole beetroots and toss in the oil mixture, making sure that the beetroot skins are all shiny. Wrap each beetroot in foil and place in a baking dish then roast for approximately 1 hour or until just tender. Peel the beetroot and cut into thick slices.

Very finely slice the fennel bulb and peel the oranges, trimming any white pith. Cut the orange into segments.

Next, make the dressing. Combine the dill, balsamic vinegar, olive oil and salt and pepper to taste and whisk well until thick.

Arrange the beetroots on a serving platter with the thinly sliced fennel and orange. Drizzle over the dill vinaigrette then scatter the crushed hazelnuts on top.

Salad of Sautéed Duck with Thyme and Honey

Indulgent and rich, this salad was a favourite dish at my Hawthorn cooking school. It is a perfect way to begin a meal featuring the flavours of the Mediterranean. I love the way honey marries beautifully with the richness of the duck.

Ingredients

3 duck breasts, skin on
salt and pepper
1 tablespoon peanut oil

2 teaspoons butter
1 sprig thyme, leaves picked from the stalk
2 tablespoons honey

1 tablespoon lemon juice
2 tablespoons walnut oil
fine grey sea salt and cracked black pepper

200g (7oz) mixed baby lettuce leaves (mesclun), washed and spun dry
1 pomegranate (optional), seeds and pulp scooped out

6 large cherry tomatoes
basil leaves to garnish

Method

Heat the oven to 190°C (370°F). Season duck breast with a little salt and pepper.

Heat peanut oil in a pan until almost smoking then add the duck breast, skin side down, and cook on a high heat until the skin is deep caramel brown. Transfer the pan containing the duck to the preheated oven until the duck is cooked rare, 7-10 minutes. (Do not turn the duck breasts over.)

Remove the pan from the oven and remove the breasts from pan, keeping them warm, and drain and discard the excess fat. Add the butter and when it begins to bubble add the thyme leaves then the honey. When simmering, replace duck breasts, skin side up.

Cook for a further minute on low heat then remove pan altogether.

Whisk together the lemon juice, walnut oil, salt and pepper and the pan juices and mix well. Toss the lettuce leaves and pomegranate through a little of the dressing.

Divide the lettuce leaves between the plates, garnish with tomatoes. Slice duck breast and arrange around the salad, drizzling any excess honey sauce over the duck slices. Garnish with basil leaves and serve.

Tuscan Panzanella with Roasted Tomato Vinaigrette

The combination of tomato and bread is delicious, and when teamed with some fresh herbs and an interesting dressing the result is sublime. It is hard to believe that this is the most basic peasant food, borne out of poverty and the need to use all ingredients at your disposal. These days, panzanella is popular throughout Italy as a light and tasty summer dish. Make sure you buy the best tomatoes available.

Ingredients

600g (21oz) stale, rustic Italian-style bread (about ½ loaf)
2 tablespoons olive oil
2 tablespoons fresh rosemary, chopped

1kg (2lb) assorted tomatoes
1 continental cucumber
1 small Spanish onion
20 kalamata olives
20 basil leaves
4 mint leaves, finely sliced
1 tablespoon fresh marjoram

Dressing:
4 small tomatoes
½ cup quality olive oil
2 tablespoons red wine vinegar
1 tablespoon balsamic vinegar
3 cloves garlic
salt and freshly ground pepper

Method

Cut the bread into cubes and toss with 2 tablespoons olive oil and the rosemary. Spread out on a baking tray and bake at 200°C (400°F) for 5 minutes until golden, then cool.

To make the dressing, heat a heavy pan and brush the skins of the small tomatoes with a little olive oil. Cook these whole tomatoes in the pan until well blackened all over. Purée with the remaining olive oil, vinegars, garlic and salt and pepper to taste. Set aside.

Remove the seeds from the other tomatoes and chop into small chunks. Peel the cucumber and remove the seeds by running a teaspoon along the central seed area. Slice finely. Finely chop the Spanish onion. Remove the stones from the olives by squashing them with the wide blade of a knife.

In a mixing bowl, place the bread cubes, tomatoes, cucumber, Spanish onion, olives and torn basil leaves. Add the chopped mint and marjoram. Mix well. Pour the dressing over and toss thoroughly. Allow to sit for 10 minutes then serve.

Warm Lima Bean and Prosciutto Salad with Rocket

Hearty and full of flavour, this typically Tuscan dish comes from the land where locals laughingly call themselves 'bean eaters' because they eat so many dried beans. If you do not like prosciutto, smoked beef also works well in this salad. Note that you must begin this recipe a day ahead, to allow time to soak the beans.

Ingredients

500g (1lb) dried lima beans

2 tablespoons olive oil
½ teaspoon dried chilli flakes
3 garlic cloves, minced
100g (3½ oz) prosciutto, roughly chopped

salt and freshly ground pepper
10 basil leaves, torn
2 handfuls of rocket leaves

Method

Place the lima beans in a large bowl of warm water and soak overnight.

The next day, drain the beans and place them in a saucepan of cold water. Bring to the boil and simmer for 1 hour or until just tender. Drain, reserving a ladle or two of the cooking water.

Heat the olive oil in a medium saucepan. Add the chilli flakes and garlic and sauté briefly until the garlic is golden. Add the prosciutto and stir over moderate heat until beginning to brown, about 2 minutes. Add the lima beans and cook, tossing occasionally, until heated through, about 3 minutes, adding some of the reserved cooking water if the mixture seems a little dry.

Season with salt and pepper and add the torn basil leaves and rocket. Toss gently then serve warm.

Warm Salad of Capsicum and Rosemary

More an antipasto choice than a salad, this delicious combination of flavours is served all over Italy with crusty bread and a good glass of local wine. It improves in flavour over a day or two, so you can make it ahead if you wish.

Ingredients

6 large capsicums of assorted colours

2 tablespoons virgin olive oil
1 large Spanish onion, peeled and cut into eights
3 tablespoons fresh rosemary
3 cloves garlic, minced

1 tablespoon balsamic vinegar
salt and freshly ground pepper to taste

Method

Slice the 4 sides off each capsicum and discard the seed core. Slice the capsicum pieces into long, thin strips.

Heat the olive oil in a frypan and add the Spanish onion and rosemary and sauté on a high heat for 3 minutes. Add the garlic and all the capsicum pieces and toss thoroughly with the rosemary flavoured oil.

Continue cooking over a low heat for 30 minutes, stirring often, until the capsicum pieces are wilted and the onion has caramelised a little. Add the balsamic vinegar and cook for a further 5 minutes.

Add salt and pepper to taste and serve warm.

Note: To turn this salad into a true antipasto, cook the capsicum/onion mixture over a medium/high heat (instead of low heat) for 30 minutes until the capsicum pieces are almost meltingly soft.

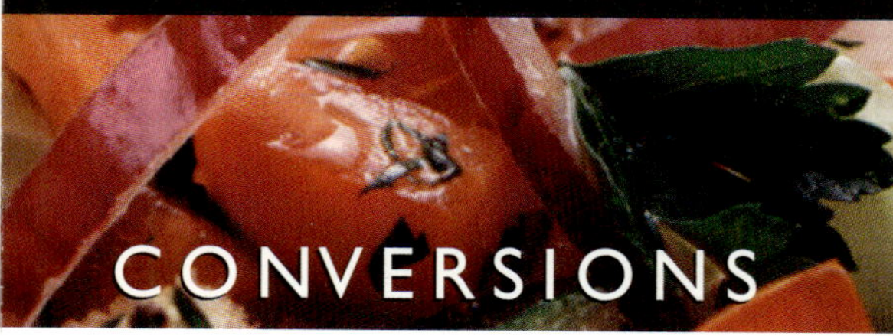

CONVERSIONS

Measurements

All cup and spoon measurements are level.

Australian		USA Equivalent	
tsp	5ml	tsp	$^1/_6$ oz
tbspn	20ml	tbspn	$^2/_3$ oz
cup	250ml	cup	8 oz
	30g		1 oz
	50g		$1^2/_3$ oz
	200g		7 oz
	250g		8 oz
	400g		14 oz
	500g		16 oz
	600g		21 oz
	700g		25 oz
	800g		28 oz
	1kg		35 oz
	100ml		$3^1/_2$ fl oz
	120ml		4 fl oz
	150ml		5 fl oz
	300ml		10 fl oz
	400ml		$13^1/_2$ fl oz
	500ml		$16^1/_2$ fl oz
	700ml		$23^1/_2$ fl oz
	800ml		$26^1/_2$ fl oz
	900ml		1 qt
	1l		33 fl oz

Length (approx.)

1cm	$^1/_3$"	5cm	2"
2cm	$^3/_4$"	15cm	6"
4cm	$1^1/_2$"	40cm	16"

GLOSSARY

beetroot: regular round beet

capsicum: bell pepper

chickpeas: garbanzos

coriander: cilantro

Desiree potatoes: winter potato with red skin, yellow flesh and oval shape

entrée: the "entry" or hors d'oeuvre in Australia or Europe; in US entrée means main course

feta: a salty, Greek-style white ewes' milk cheese

ghee: clarified butter

jam: jelly in the US

julienne: vegetables cut into thin strips

mirin: Japanese sweet, syrupy rice wine

prawn: shrimp

punnet: small basket ~ 8 oz

Roma tomatoes: sauce tomatoes

shallots: French eschallots

Spanish onion: purple onion

Splenda®: artificial sweetener, maltodextrin and sucralose, as sweet as sugar gram for gram

spring onions: scallions

sugar snaps: snap peas with edible pods

See page 126 for a full-page glossary.

Temperatures

160°C	320°F	200°C	390°F
170°C	330°F	210°C	410°F
180°C	350°F	220°C	430°F
190°C	370°F	250°C	480°F

If you have enjoyed the innovation, variety and delicious flavours of any one of Tamara's fantastic cookbooks, you should try others in the series—you most certainly will not be disappointed. Listed below is a brief synopsis of each of her books.

***B**ake Your Cake and Eat It Too presents a mouthwatering variety of cakes, both sweet and savoury. Tamara's easy-to-follow recipes will have you baking up a storm, creating cakes that will soon become family favourites. From the Asian-influenced Chinese Ginger Syrup Cake to the savoury Eggplant and Goat Cheese Cake, there is a recipe to suit any occasion, to follow any meal or to satisfy the most discerning tastebud.*

***S**tuff It! the art of creating filled food: why not try your hand at the art of creating filled food with Tamara's fantastic book. Filled Italian pasta, Mexican street foods, Asian rice paper rolls and Indian samosas—create a startling array of marvellous finger foods which tantalise the tastebuds.*

***R**isotto 'round the world features modern-flavoured risottos which incorporate taste-tantalising ingredients in wonderful recipes from all four corners of the earth. While they remain true to the traditional method of making risotto, they allow the flavours of exotic ingredients to share the limelight.*

***S**oup! simply soul in a bowl: this wonderfully versatile cookbook features hearty soups to nourish and satisfy, as well as light and refreshing soups which can be served either hot or chilled. Complete with a range of low-fat soups, which don't taste low-fat at all.*

***S**alads! the art of creating cool food: in this book Tamara has created a beautiful range of salads from around the world. From Australia to Zambia, you can experience the best the world has to offer. Try Couscous Salad with Seafood and Fresh Mint or Warm Mediterranean Salsa of Eggplant, Tomato and Roasted Garlic or, for the more traditional, the best Caesar salad you will ever try.*

***B**reads! Tamara's original cooking classes were based on bread cooking. We now find that more and more home cooks are baking their own bread, some using new electric bread makers whilst others are prepared to bake by the traditional method. This book covers all areas, with some of the best-tasting breads you will ever bake. From flat breads to sweet breads, you will have a great deal of enjoyment using the tried and true recipes Tamara has included in this book.*

If you have any difficulty in obtaining a copy of any of the above titles, just contact the publisher at the address below: R&R Publications Marketing Pty Ltd, PO Box 254, Carlton North, Victoria 3054, Australia.

Telephone (03) 9381 2199 Fax (03) 9381 2689, or call our National Toll-free number: 1 800 063 296. E-mail:richardc@bigpond.net.au

Warm Tomato Gratin Salad

Tomatoes bought in summer or autumn will always have more flavour and sweetness than those bought out of season, and this recipe really allows the summer flavours to shine. If you grow your own tomatoes, this recipe will give you even greater results.

Ingredients

2 tablespoons melted butter
2 tablespoons olive oil
2 cups fresh breadcrumbs
½ cup chopped parsley
20 large basil leaves, finely sliced
½ bunch chives, chopped
salt and cracked black pepper to taste

6-8 large tomatoes

200g (7oz) assorted mixed lettuce leaves
2 tablespoons olive oil
1 tablespoon balsamic vinegar
salt and pepper to taste

Method

Heat the butter and olive oil in a large frypan and add the breadcrumbs, parsley, basil and chives and toss until golden. Add salt and pepper to taste.

Thickly slice the tomatoes and place them on a non-stick oven tray, adding salt and pepper to taste, then press the crumb mixture over the tomatoes to cover each slice.

Bake the tomatoes at 180°C (350°F) for 10 minutes then grill just to toast the crumbs.

Meanwhile, toss the lettuce leaves with the combined olive oil and vinegar and add salt and pepper to taste.

Arrange the lettuce leaves on a platter then top with the tomato slices, allowing each to overlap the previous one. Grind freshly black pepper over and serve.

Salads of India and the Subcontinent

There is no end to the flavours and textures of Indian cooking. While many of us interpret 'curry' as an indication of Indian cuisine, in truth, the vast and varied cuisine of India and the subcontinent provides a never-ending array of flavour and texture combinations to enjoy.

Some salads in this chapter are modern interpretations of traditional-style dishes, since most Indian salads are simple combinations of vegetables designed to enhance more complex hot dishes.

You will find that the traditional dahl (lentils) makes a fantastic salad base and, as well as being incredibly healthy, they also adopt other flavours well. Chickpeas and rice also feature, while Indian spices work their magic on chicken and lamb to create wonderfully flavoured main course salads.

Indian Coconut Rice Salad

This dish is a modern version of a typical Indian rice pilaf that would be served as an everyday accompaniment to a curry. If you wish to make this dish more luxurious, use basmati rice instead of the regular long grain.

Ingredients

350g (12oz) long grain rice

60g (2oz) ghee
100g (3½oz) coconut threads
100g (3½oz) cashews

1 teaspoon black mustard seeds
5 curry leaves
2 teaspoons black lentils*

1 large onion, finely chopped
3 cloves garlic, minced
1 teaspoon turmeric
½-1 teaspoon chilli powder
salt
225ml (7½oz) coconut milk
600ml (20oz) water, approx.

Method

Wash the rice well under cold water then soak in more cold water for 1 hour. Drain well.

Heat 1 tablespoon of the ghee in a sauté pan, add the coconut and cashews and toast in the pan until golden, then remove and set aside.

Heat the remaining 2 tablespoons of ghee in the same pan and add the mustard seeds, sliced curry leaves and black lentils. Stir and cook until fragrant. Add the finely chopped onion and minced garlic and continue cooking until the onion has softened. Add the turmeric, chilli, salt and coconut milk and simmer for 5 minutes.

Add the drained rice and 600ml (20oz) water and stir well. Cover and simmer until the rice is tender. Lift the lid, stir gently and taste to check whether the rice has cooked. If it is still a little firm, add some more water and simmer until all the liquid is absorbed. Cool.

Add half the coconut and cashews and stir through to distribute then garnish with the remaining coconut and cashew mixture and serve immediately.

*Other lentils can be substituted if black ones are not available.

Indian Chickpea Salad with Spinach

(photographed on page 65)

Chickpeas are a primary source of fibre in India and turn up in all sorts of wonderful dishes. This salad is a fabulous option when entertaining outdoors, or when you need to make a salad to transport to a barbecue as it travels very well. Take care not to overcook the chickpeas or they will disintegrate.

Serves 8

Ingredients

2 cups dry chickpeas
4 onions
1 teaspoon whole cloves
4 bay leaves

60ml (2oz) peanut or olive oil
4 cloves garlic
1 teaspoon turmeric
2 teaspoons cumin
2 teaspoons garam masala

3 tablespoons tomato paste
2 red capsicums, sliced

4 medium zucchini, sliced on the diagonal
salt and pepper to taste
2 bunches of spinach or 500g (1lb) baby spinach

Method

Pick over the chickpeas and remove any that are discoloured. Place all remaining chickpeas in a large saucepan and cover with cold water. Peel 2 of the onions and chop in half. Place these in the saucepan with the chickpeas. Add the cloves and bay leaves and bring to the boil and simmer for 10 minutes then remove the chickpeas from the heat and cover and allow to 'steep' for 2 hours. Strain the chickpeas discarding the onions, cloves and bay leaves, reserving some of the soaking water.

Chop the remaining 2 onions. Heat the oil and sauté the onions and the minced garlic. Add all the spices and cook briefly to release their fragrance. Add the soaked chickpeas and 2 cups of the soaking water, the tomato paste and the red capsicum strips.

Cover and simmer gently for about 20 minutes until the chickpeas soften and the liquid evaporates. Add the zucchini and salt and pepper to taste and stir well then remove from the heat. Allow to cool slightly then fold through the spinach leaves.

Cool completely and serve.

*Never add salt to pulses until after the initial cooking or soaking because the salt will toughen the skin of the bean and inhibit its ability to absorb liquid.

Indian Salad of Spiced Chicken and Dahl (Lentils)

Indian flavours lend themselves fabulously well to main course salads. Spicing the meat before cooking adds flavour and interest.

Serves 6-8

Ingredients

6 cups vegetable stock
1½ cups dried lentils
juice of 2 lemons
40ml (1⅓ oz) vegetable oil

1 tablespoon curry powder
1 tablespoon garam masala
1 teaspoon turmeric

salt and pepper to taste
4 large chicken breast fillets, skin removed

1½ cups vegetable stock, extra
1 small cauliflower, cut into florets
1½ cups fresh or frozen peas

2 small tomatoes, seeded, diced

1 cucumber, peeled and diced
2 green onions, sliced
2 tablespoons chopped fresh mint
salt and pepper to taste

2 large bunches watercress, trimmed
fresh mint, extra, for garnish
spring onion greens, for garnish

Method

Bring 6 cups of vegetable stock to the boil and add the lentils. Simmer until the lentils are tender, but still retain their shape, about 20 minutes. Drain well then transfer the lentils to a large bowl and add the lemon juice and 1 tablespoon of the oil. Mix well, cover and chill.

Combine the curry powder, garam masala and turmeric in a plastic bag with salt and pepper to taste then add the chicken breasts to the bag. Seal the bag and shake vigorously, allowing the spices to coat the chicken breasts evenly. Heat a grill pan or non-stick frypan with the remaining oil until smoking then add the chicken breasts to the pan until golden brown and cooked through on both sides, about 5 minutes. Remove the chicken and set aside.

To the used pan, add the extra 1½ cups of stock and bring to the boil. Add the cauliflower and peas and cook over high heat until vegetables are crisp-tender and most of liquid has evaporated, about 5 minutes. Add this vegetable mixture to the lentils and mix well. Add the diced tomatoes, diced cucumber, sliced spring onions and chopped fresh mint and mix well, adding salt and pepper to taste.

Slice the chicken into diagonal strips then gently mix these into the salad. Arrange the watercress on a platter and top with the salad mixture, arranging so that there is plenty of chicken visible. Garnish with fresh mint and spring onion greens.

Pakistani Green Bean Salad with Coriander and Ginger

Snake beans are a common vegetable in India and Pakistan and are wonderful in this salad because they retain their 'crunch' after cooking. If you cannot find them, use common green beans but reduce the stock and cooking time accordingly.

Ingredients

700g (1½ lb) fresh snake beans
2cm (¾") piece fresh ginger

1 tablespoon vegetable oil
1 tablespoon sesame oil
1 teaspoon mustard seeds

2 teaspoons ground cumin
½ teaspoon turmeric
1 fresh green chilli, finely minced

150ml (5oz) chicken/vegetable stock
juice of 2 lemons
1 bunch fresh coriander, washed, dried then chopped
salt to taste
80g (3oz) peanuts, roasted and chopped

Method

Trim the beans to lengths of 8cm (3") and discard any discoloured ends. Peel the ginger and cut into fine matchsticks (julienne).

Heat a wok with the vegetable and sesame oils and, when hot, add the mustard seeds. Allow them to cook for a moment or two until they start popping. Add the ginger and cook for a further minute. Add the ground cumin, turmeric and chilli and stir until fragrant, 2 minutes.

Add all the beans and toss in the flavoured oil to coat them thoroughly. Add the stock, cover and simmer for 5-8 minutes or until the liquid has almost evaporated completely, and the beans are tender.

Remove the lid and add the lemon juice, coriander and salt to taste. Stir thoroughly to combine all the ingredients then cool. Serve garnished with roasted chopped peanuts and, if desired, lemon wedges.

Tandoori Lamb Salad with Black Onion Seeds and Sesame

I love the complex flavours and textures of Indian cooking. The mixture of spices, sometimes subtle and sometimes robust, seems to linger on the palate long after the meal has been enjoyed which heightens the pleasure for me. This salad contains all the interest of a traditional Indian meal but in a more modern style.

Serves 6

Ingredients

For the marinade: 1 large onion, chopped
20g (²⁄₃ oz) piece fresh ginger, grated
juice of 1 fresh lemon
1 tablespoon water
½ cup plain yoghurt
2 teaspoons ground coriander
2 teaspoons ground cumin
½ teaspoon ground turmeric
¼ teaspoon cayenne
1 tablespoon garam masala
¼ teaspoon mace
1 teaspoon salt

For the salad: 12 large lamb cutlets
1 cup sesame seeds
½ cup black onion seeds*

250g (8oz) baby spinach leaves
200g (7oz) mixed baby lettuce leaves (mesclun)
4 spring onions, sliced
40ml (1⅓ oz) white vinegar
60ml (2oz) peanut oil
few drops toasted sesame oil
salt and pepper to taste

Method

Place the onion, ginger, lemon juice and water in a food processor with the yoghurt, spices and salt and process until the mixture is smooth. Remove from the processor and pour over the lamb cutlets, turning to coat both sides of the lamb. Marinate for a minimum of 4 hours or up to 8 hours.

Preheat the oven to 220°C (430°F). When you are ready to cook, mix the sesame seeds and onion seeds together and place them on a plate. Remove the lamb cutlets from the marinade one at a time, allowing the excess marinade to run off then dip each cutlet in the sesame mixture, coating both sides. Place the coated cutlets on a non-stick baking tray and bake in the preheated oven for 10 minutes for medium rare, or longer if you prefer.

Meanwhile, prepare the salad. Wash and dry the spinach and mixed lettuce leaves and place them, with the spring onions, in a large salad bowl. Whisk together the vinegar and oil with salt and pepper to taste then add the few drops of sesame oil, continuing to whisk until the dressing is thick. Toss the salad with the dressing until the leaves are well coated then divide the salad between 6 plates. Arrange 2 cutlets on each plate and serve immediately.

*Black onion seeds (nigella) are available from Indian grocery stores. If unavailable, simple use extra sesame seeds.

Salads of the Americas

The Americas is such a vast area with so many food traditions and styles. This chapter touches on the food of the United States with a delicious salad of chicken marinated in a combination of mustard and molasses with a touch of honey.

Recipes in this chapter have a strong leaning toward the diverse and exciting food of Mexico, with salads of roasted corn or perhaps a beguiling salad of jîcama, tortilla strips, toasted pumpkin seeds and coriander. Of course, chillies feature, but you can use them to suit your tastebuds.

The Pacific Rim has had a huge influence on global cuisine over the last few years, so some of these recipes feature an 'east-west' theme. Try the seared tuna with crisp wontons and a citrus dressing or sesame prawn salad with mango and crunchy coconut.

Remember that, as with all cooking, the end result can only be as good as the quality of the ingredients, so buy fresh ingredients from a reputable supplier.

Chargrilled Coconut Prawns with Soba Noodles

King prawns are a real luxury but, since they are rich, a little goes quite a long way. Two or three for each person is usually sufficient. I always buy them peeled with the tails left on for maximum convenience. Experiment with other seafood such as scallops, squid or salmon.

Serves 6

Ingredients

500g (1lb) soba noodles

200g (7oz) coconut milk or coconut cream
1 small hot red chilli, seeded and minced
1 teaspoon fresh ginger, minced
10 fresh basil leaves, shredded
½ bunch fresh coriander

400-500g (1lb) raw (green) king prawns
2 tablespoons peanut oil

2 tablespoons sesame seeds

Dressing: 2 tablespoons sweet chilli sauce
2 tablespoons sesame oil
3 tablespoons vegetable stock
1 teaspoon sugar
1 tablespoon soy sauce
salt and pepper to taste

Method

Cook the noodles according to packet instructions, until firm but tender. Meanwhile, mix the dressing ingredients adding salt and pepper to taste. Drain the noodles and toss with the dressing while still warm.

Mix the coconut milk with the chilli, ginger, basil and half the coriander and allow to marinate for 10 minutes.

Brush the prawns with the peanut oil and chargrill or grill until coloured orange and just cooked through. As soon as they are grilled, remove from the grill and plunge into the coconut milk mixture.

Remove the prawns from the marinade. Arrange the noodles on individual serving platters, top with the prawns and spoon a small amount of the coconut marinade over.

Sprinkle with remaining coriander and sesame seeds and serve.

My Favourite Caesar Salad

(photographed on page 75)

Most people aren't aware of the unusual history of this most popular salad. History tells us that in 1930 a young and penniless Italian chef named Caesar Cardini travelled to Mexico to work and began to make his salad in a restaurant in Tijuana. Word spread and business for the restaurant boomed. Four years later the young chef bought the restaurant, and today the restaurant still serves the traditional salad prepared at the table. There are dozens of different versions of this salad, with heated discussion about what makes the best 'Caesar'—this is my favourite!

Ingredients

2 cloves garlic, minced
4 tablespoons olive oil

9 slices anchovies
juice of 1½ lemons
a good dash of Worcestershire sauce
dash of prepared mustard
1-2 tablespoons white wine vinegar

4 eggs, boiled for 1 minute (yolks only)

2 thick slices country bread
2 tablespoons olive oil
salt and pepper to taste

100g (3½ oz) prosciutto

3 heads of romaine or cos lettuce
5-6 tablespoons Parmesan cheese
freshly ground pepper

Method

Preheat the oven to 220°C (430°F).

In a large mixing bowl, place the minced garlic and olive oil and, using the base of a metal spoon, squash and pound the garlic into the oil. Add the anchovies and mash these into the oil mixture. Whisk in the lemon juice then Worcestershire sauce, mustard and white wine vinegar, mixing thoroughly to incorporate each ingredient before the next is added.

Crack the eggs carefully after they have been boiled for 1 minute then discard the whites and add the yolks to the mixing bowl. Mix these in thoroughly, incorporating them into the other ingredients. Set aside.

Cut the bread into cubes and toss with the olive oil and salt and pepper. Transfer to a baking tray and bake the cubes until golden, about 15 minutes. Cool.

Crisp the prosciutto in a frypan or microwave then break into smaller pieces.

Place the well-washed lettuce leaves in a mixing bowl and toss them thoroughly in the dressing for several minutes until all the leaves have been coated. Add the bread cubes, Parmesan cheese, and finish with black pepper and crisp prosciutto.

Serve immediately.

Roasted Corn and Bean Salad Mexicana

I love this salad. It looks so summery and is a good side dish for strong flavours like lamb or game. It is best on the day it is made to preserve the roasted aroma, but still tastes quite good a day or two later.

Ingredients

4 ears of corn
2 red capsicums, chopped
1 green capsicum, chopped

1 Spanish onion, chopped
1 tablespoon paprika
1 tablespoon ground cumin

2 tablespoons oil
2 cloves garlic, minced
6 yellow squash
400g (14oz) can lima beans, rinsed
400g (14oz) can red kidney beans, rinsed
120ml (4oz) vegetable stock
1 teaspoon Tabasco sauce
1 teaspoon sugar or Splenda®

juice of 2 limes
½ cup fresh coriander, chopped
salt and pepper to taste

Method

Cut the corn from the ears and remove and discard the seed core from the capsicums.

In a large non-stick pan, add the chopped Spanish onion, chopped red and green capsicum flesh, paprika, cumin and the corn and cook over a high heat until the vegetables begin to blacken and blister, stirring often. Remove from the pan and set aside.

Add the oil, garlic and squash to the used pan and cook for 4 minutes, stirring constantly.

Add the lima beans, kidney beans, stock, Tabasco and sugar and cook until the liquid has evaporated and the vegetables are hot.

Remove from the heat and add lime juice, fresh coriander and salt and pepper to taste. Add the corn mixture and toss thoroughly to coat all the vegetables.

Serve warm or at room temperature.

Rock Lobster and Smoked Ocean Trout Salad

Fish and shellfish salads make perfect summer meals. You can substitute different types of fish and shellfish to change the flavour of the salad to suit your tastes, making this a recipe for all seasons.

Serves 6

Ingredients

1 cooked rock lobster
400g (14oz) smoked ocean trout

1 continental cucumber
1 carrot
1 green zucchini
1 yellow zucchini

100g (3½ oz) tatsoi leaves

1 bunch chives, snipped

Dressing:

juice of 2 limes
1 tablespoon palm sugar
½ cup olive oil
salt and pepper

Method

Remove the meat from the tail of the rock lobster, slice finely and set aside. Alternatively ask your fishmonger to do this for you. Cut the smoked ocean trout into thin strips and also set aside.

Slice the cucumber in half, lengthways and scoop out and discard the seeds. Slice on a mandoline or 'V- slicer' (or use a vegetable peeler) to make long, skinny strips resembling fettuccine. Peel the carrot and slice in the same manner as the cucumber. Keeping the zucchini whole, also slice them lengthways into long thin strips.

Mix the lobster, ocean trout, vegetables and tatsoi leaves gently.

For the dressing, heat the lime juice and dissolve the palm sugar. Pour into a bowl and whisk in the olive oil until the mixture is thick and the oil has emulsified with the lime juice. Season with salt and pepper and mix this through the salad ingredients.

Arrange the salad in an attractive platter and sprinkle the chives over.

Seared Tuna Salad with Crisp Wontons

Pacific Rim flavours are now so much a part of our cuisine, it is hard to remember a time when we didn't take them for granted. This salad brings so many flavours and textures together to create a delicious main course salad.

Ingredients

Dressing:
½ cup olive oil
60ml (2oz) fresh lime juice
60ml (2oz) orange juice
50ml (1⅔ oz) soy sauce
50ml (1⅔ oz) rice vinegar
20ml (⅔ oz) toasted sesame oil
½ bunch fresh chives, minced
1 tablespoon fresh ginger, minced
salt and pepper to taste

Salad:
1-2 tablespoons peanut oil
1 small red chilli, minced
8 spring onions, finely sliced on the diagonal
100g (3½ oz) baby corn
150g (5oz) snow peas, trimmed

4 tablespoons sesame seeds
4 tablespoons black onion seeds (nigella)
4 x 150g (4 x 5oz) tuna steaks
salt and pepper to taste

vegetable oil (for deep-frying)
8 wonton wrappers, cut into thin strips

250g (8oz) mixed baby lettuce leaves (mesclun)

Method

First, make the dressing. Whisk olive oil, lime juice, orange juice, soy sauce, rice vinegar, sesame oil, chives and ginger in small bowl to blend. Season with salt and pepper.

Heat a little oil in a frypan or wok and add the chilli, spring onions, baby corn and snow peas, tossing over a high heat until the vegetables are crisp tender, about 3 minutes. Transfer the hot vegetables to a bowl and drizzle over a little of the dressing. Set aside.

Mix the sesame seeds and black onion seeds on a flat plate and season the fish with salt and pepper. Press the fish into the seed mixture, coating both sides evenly. Heat a little more oil in the same frypan used for the vegetables. Add the tuna and sear over a high heat until the fish is just cooked through. Transfer to a platter and, when cool, use a sharp knife to slice each fillet thinly.

To prepare the wontons, heat some vegetable oil in a wok or frypan and, when smoking, add the strips of wonton and cook until golden brown. Remove from the pan and drain on absorbent paper. Add salt to taste.

Toss the lettuce leaves with the cooked vegetable mixture and a little more dressing, tossing thoroughly so that the leaves are well coated. Add salt and pepper to taste. Divide the lettuce mixture between 4 plates and top with the sliced, seared tuna slices. Arrange a bundle of fried wonton strips on top.

Sesame Coconut King Prawns with Mango Salsa

Elegant and with assertive flavours, this salad makes a perfect entrée or light summer lunch. Most of the preparation can be done ahead, making this quick and easy to assemble.

Serves 4

Ingredients

12 raw king prawns, peeled, with tail left on
salt and pepper to taste
flour for dusting
1 egg, beaten
1 cup sesame seeds
1 cup coconut threads

1 mango, peeled and finely diced
½ small Spanish onion, very finely diced
2 tablespoons coriander, chopped
juice of 1 lime

2 tablespoons butter or olive oil
assorted greens of your choice

Method

Butterfly the prawns along the inner curve then dust with salt and pepper and flour. Dip in egg, allowing the excess to run off then dredge in a mixture of sesame seeds and coconut. Set aside.

Mix the diced mango, onion, coriander and lime juice in a bowl and season to taste.

Heat the butter or olive oil in a frypan, add the king prawns and fry over a high heat for 1-2 minutes each side until golden. (You may need to apply pressure with a spatula as they cook to prevent them from curling up.)

To serve, arrange some leaves on each plate and top with 3 cooked prawns and a generous spoonful of the mango salsa.

Drizzle over any remaining salsa juice and serve immediately with lime wedges if desired.

Tortilla Salad Mexicana

Spicy and sweet, this unusual salad is full of interesting flavours and textures. Make it just before serving for best results.

Ingredients

Dressing:
- 1 small mango, peeled, pitted, diced
- ½ cup grapefruit juice
- ¼ cup fresh lime juice
- 1-2 small red chillies
- 4 shallots, chopped
- 30ml (1oz) vegetable oil
- 1 garlic clove

Salad:
- oil for frying
- 4 corn tortillas, cut into strips

- 3 cups thinly sliced green cabbage
- 3 cups thinly sliced iceberg lettuce
- 1 mango, peeled and flesh diced
- 1 cup diced, peeled jîcama
- 1 red or purple onion, finely diced
- 3 red capsicums, roasted, peeled and sliced
- ½ cup shelled pumpkin seeds, toasted
- ½ bunch coriander, chopped
- salt and pepper to taste

Method

First, make the dressing. Place all the ingredients in a blender or food processor and blend until smooth. Set aside.

Next, make the salad. Heat oil in heavy medium saucepan over medium-high heat.

Add a handful of tortilla strips and cook until crisp, about 4 minutes per batch, then remove from the oil and drain on absorbent paper.

Combine cabbage, lettuce, mango, jîcama, onion, capsicums, pumpkin seeds and coriander in a large bowl. Toss with enough dressing to coat, adding salt and pepper to taste. Add the tortilla and serve.

Warm Salad of Mustard-glazed Chicken with Red Wine Vinaigrette

This is one of the best chicken dishes I have eaten. It is simple to create with wonderful flavours that are incredibly versatile. The chicken can marinate for several hours then requires a simple period of cooking unattended in the oven, making this a perfect recipe for entertaining.

Ingredients

3 tablespoons mustard seeds
3 tablespoons malt vinegar
2 tablespoons honey
1 tablespoon molasses
1 tablespoon brown sugar
½ cup olive oil
4 tablespoons French mustard
2 cloves garlic, minced
½ cup boiling water

8 skinless chicken breast fillets

2 tablespoons red or white wine vinegar
2 tablespoons olive oil
salt and pepper to taste

300g (10½ oz) assorted baby lettuce leaves (mesclun), well washed and dried
300g (10½ oz) baby spinach leaves, well washed and dried
1 bunch spring onions, sliced on the diagonal
1 bunch chives, chopped

Method

Make the marinade. Ground 2 tablespoons of the mustard seeds into powder, then mix the ground seeds with the malt vinegar, honey, molasses, brown sugar, olive oil, French mustard, garlic and boiling water. Whisk well until the mixture is thick and smooth.

Reserve 4 tablespoons of marinade for later use. Lay the chicken in a flat glass dish and pour the remaining marinade over. Turn the chicken so that both sides of the chicken are covered in the marinade and chill for a minimum of 4 hours.

Remove the chicken from the marinade, making sure that each piece of chicken has a good coating of the marinating mixture. Place in an ovenproof baking dish or on an oven tray and bake at 210°C (410°F) for 20-25 minutes, until cooked through.

Meanwhile, transfer the reserved marinade to a saucepan and bring to the boil. Simmer for 5 minutes then remove from the heat. Remove the chicken from the oven and keep warm.

Make a dressing with the red or white wine vinegar and olive oil with salt and pepper to taste and a little of the reserved warm marinade. Whisk well. Toss some dressing through the mixed lettuce and spinach leaves just to coat them (do not use too much). Add the spring onions and chopped chives and toss again.

To serve, arrange the salad leaves on plates then top each mound of salad with a chicken breast, sliced on the diagonal. Drizzle around a little remaining warm marinade.

Salads with Modern Flavours

As ingredients from all over the world flood our supermarkets and food stores, we have become very confident in the kitchen. There are all sorts of dishes and recipes that we have created that fall into no specific geographic region, but that are bursting with modern flavour combinations.

This chapter features my favourite salads that have been created with good taste and fine produce in mind. All of them evolved after visits to markets where I purchased seasonal vegetables and fruits and then brought them home to experiment. After a few additional ingredients from my refrigerator and pantry were added, the salads began to take shape.

I adore the flavour of roasted sweet potato and when it is mixed with chopped sweet onion, coriander and a little fresh chilli, the flavour combination is sublime. Chopped peanuts add crunch and complete the salad in the most delicious way.

Slightly bitter watercress is a natural partner for firm autumn pears, and some cracked black pepper and a tart vinaigrette makes this salad irresistible. Wild rice is a healthy grain which marries perfectly with toasted nuts and herbs.

While cooking inspiration comes from travel, eating out and reading, it should also come from within. So when you are next at the market and faced with some fantastic seasonal produce, why not do as I do and buy a kilo or two of whatever takes your fancy then bring it home and create something fantastic all your own.

Grilled Vegetable Salad

This nutritious salad will partner any main course beautifully. Any leftovers can be chopped more finely and added to a pasta sauce or pizza.

Ingredients

2 medium eggplants, cut into quarters
salt

1 tablespoon chopped fresh rosemary
$\frac{1}{4}$ teaspoon freshly ground black pepper
2 tablespoons olive oil
3 tablespoons red wine vinegar
juice of 1 large lemon
2 cloves garlic, minced

vegetable cooking spray
3 ears fresh corn, husked
3 small zucchini, cut on the diagonal
3 small yellow squash, thickly sliced
2 large red bell pepper, cut into thick slices
1 Spanish onion, sliced thickly
1 large, unpeeled tomato, quartered

salt and pepper to taste

Method

Thickly slice the eggplants and generously salt the surface. Allow the eggplants to drain for 30 minutes then wash and dry quickly.

Combine the rosemary, black pepper, olive oil, vinegar, lemon juice and garlic and whisk well. Brush ears of corn and the cut surfaces of the other vegetables with half of olive oil mixture and set aside. Reserve remaining dressing.

Coat a barbecue, grill pan or griller tray with cooking spray and preheat. Place vegetables, cut sides down, on the grill-pan, barbecue or griller and cook for 5 minutes. Brush with remaining olive oil mixture and turn vegetables over, and cook an additional 10 minutes or until tender and charred around the edges.

Alternatively, mix the vegetables with the flavoured oil and place all the vegetables in a large ovenproof baking dish. Bake at 220°C (430°F) for 40 minutes, tossing halfway through the cooking time.

To serve, cut each ear of corn into 6 pieces then mix all the vegetables together in a bowl with any remaining dressing. Toss well and season to taste with salt and freshly ground pepper. Serve hot, warm or cold.

Asparagus and Baby Green Beans with Hazelnut Dressing

(photographed on page 91)

The lovely colour of this vibrant salad is what first impresses you, but as soon as you taste it you will keep coming back for more of the delicious, healthy flavours.

Serves 8-10 as an entrée

Ingredients

Dressing:
50ml ($1\frac{2}{3}$ oz) lemon juice
50ml ($1\frac{2}{3}$ oz) white wine vinegar
3 egg yolks
1 cup hazelnut oil (or any other nut-flavoured oil)
2 tablespoons of chopped dill
1 cup chopped toasted hazelnuts

Salad:
6 bunches of asparagus, trimmed
1kg (2lb) baby green beans, topped and tailed
2 red capsicum, finely julienned

Method

To make the dressing, combine the lemon juice, vinegar and egg yolks in a food processor and blend until pale and creamy. Slowly drizzle in the oil until the dressing comes together. Stir in the chopped dill and toasted nuts and season to taste.

Bring a large saucepan of water to the boil and lower the asparagus and beans and simmer for approximately 1-2 minutes until the vegetables are just tender.

Drain and toss with the dressing, nuts and finely sliced capsicum and serve on the same day.

Sweet Potato and Peanut Salad

This lovely salad is quite filling and any leftovers make a great sandwich accompaniment . . . if you're lucky enough to have any left over. Use any sweet potato variety you like, or try using pumpkin instead.

Serves 8 as a side dish

Ingredients

2kg (4lb) sweet potato, peeled
6 tablespoons olive oil
20 cloves garlic, unpeeled
salt and pepper

1 Spanish onion, minced
1-2 small red chillies, minced
½ cup fresh herbs of your choice: e.g. coriander,
parsley, dill, chives or a mixture

2 tablespoons balsamic vinegar
2 cups roasted peanuts
salt and freshly ground pepper to taste

Method

Peel and cut the sweet potato into large chunks. Toss with 2 tablespoons of the olive oil and place in a large baking dish with the garlic cloves. Season to taste with salt and pepper and bake at 220°C (430°F) for about 1 hour or until the sweet potato is tender and golden around the edges. Remove from the oven and keep warm.

Mix the Spanish onion and minced chilli with the fresh herbs and combine with the sweet potato.

Whisk the remaining 4 tablespoons olive oil with the balsamic vinegar and toss with the sweet potato mixture. Add the peanuts, toss once more and serve. Season to taste then serve with extra herb sprigs.

Summer Salad of Grilled Chicken, Spinach and Mango

This fresh 'main course' salad is bursting with flavour while still being incredibly healthy. It is finished with a mixed nut medley, adding texture and flavour.

Serves 6

Ingredients

Salad:
- 6 Roma tomatoes
- 10 basil leaves
- 10 mint leaves
- salt and pepper
- ½ teaspoon sugar
- 12 tiny chicken fillets (from breasts)
- 1 bunch of asparagus
- 1 avocado
- 1 bunch of spring onions
- 8 firm button mushrooms
- 2 firm mangoes
- 3 large handfuls of baby spinach leaves
- ½ cup toasted hazelnuts, lightly crushed
- ½ cup toasted brazil nuts, lightly crushed
- ½ cup toasted pistachios, lightly crushed

Dressing:
- 2 teaspoons honey
- 2 tablespoons balsamic vinegar
- 3 tablespoons raspberry vinegar
- 2 tablespoons soy sauce
- 2 teaspoons Dijon mustard
- 2 teaspoons minced ginger
- 2 cloves garlic, minced
- 1 teaspoon sambal oelek (chilli paste)
- 2 tablespoons lemon juice
- 2 tablespoons olive oil (optional)
- salt and freshly ground pepper

Method

Slice the tomatoes in half lengthways, and top with sliced basil, mint, salt, pepper and sugar. Bake at 160°C (320°F) for 2 hours.

In a large jug, whisk together all the dressing ingredients until emulsified (thickened).

Marinate the chicken in ½ cup of dressing, reserving the remainder for later. Allow the chicken to marinate for 1 hour minimum (or up to 4 hours). Heat a non-stick grill pan and cook the chicken fillets over a high heat until cooked through, 2-3 minutes on each side. Transfer the cooked fillets to a plate and keep warm.

Steam, microwave or boil the asparagus until tender then refresh under cold water.

Halve the avocado, peel, and dice the flesh. Slice the spring onions diagonally and thinly slice the mushrooms. Dice the mango flesh.

To make the salad, place the well-washed spinach leaves in a large bowl and add the blanched asparagus, sliced spring onions, mushrooms and roasted tomatoes, cut into quarters. Add the reserved dressing and toss thoroughly.

Divide the salad evenly amongst individual plates and add some mango and avocado cubes. Top with 2 fillets of chicken, and a generous sprinkling of nut medley. Serve immediately.

Watercress and Pear Salad

One of the most fabulous combinations of flavours, watercress and pear marry beautifully together, with the bitterness of the leaves bouncing off the sweetness of the fruit. A little shaved Parmesan and an acidic dressing completes this perfect picture!

Serves 6-8

Ingredients

2 bunches of watercress, picked and washed

3 tablespoons olive oil
1 tablespoon lemon juice
$\frac{1}{2}$ tablespoon white wine vinegar
salt and pepper

3 beurre bosc pears, finely sliced

shavings of Parmesan

Method

Wash and dry the watercress well.

Whisk the olive oil, lemon juice and white wine vinegar with salt and pepper until the mixture has thickened slightly.

Slice pears finely and combine with watercress in a bowl.

Drizzle over dressing just enough to coat the leaves. Place on a platter and top with shavings of Parmesan.

Low Fat Salads

As someone who is constantly fighting a 'Battle of the Bulge', I have spent most of my life facing uninspiring bowls of lettuce, tomato and other raw vegetables which, when arranged together, were always called 'salad'. I always thought of salad as a necessary evil, but these days things are very different!

How lucky we are these days to have a cuisine so heavily influenced by exciting ingredients from all over the world. Now we can pick and choose unusual ingredients that contain little or no fat to create inspiring and stimulating salads to enjoy all year 'round with no feelings of deprivation at all.

This chapter was written especially for those who feel that low fat food is boring and uninspiring, but will also stimulate the palates of those who simply prefer to eat a healthy diet.

Warm Mediterranean Salad of Eggplant, Tomato and Roasted Garlic

The sunny flavours of this warm salad will remind you of the sun-drenched foods of the Mediterranean. Although light, this salad is full of interesting flavours and textures.

Serves 6

Ingredients

2 medium eggplants, diced
salt

2 small hot red chillies
1 bulb garlic
1kg (2lb) tomatoes, quartered

1 teaspoon honey
1 tablespoon balsamic vinegar
2 tablespoons olive oil
salt and freshly ground pepper to taste

500g (1lb) cooked cannellini or kidney beans*

2 tablespoons fresh chopped parsley
2 tablespoons fresh chopped chives

Method

Preheat oven to 170°C (340°F). Cut the eggplant into large dice and sprinkle with salt all over. Allow the eggplant to drain in a colander for 30 minutes then rinse away the bitter juices and dry thoroughly.

Make 2 or 3 deep cuts in each chilli. Cut the top off the bulb of garlic. Place the eggplant cubes and tomato quarters in a large baking dish with the chillies and the garlic bulb. In a small cup, mix the honey, balsamic vinegar and oil and heat until warm. Drizzle this mixture over the vegetables and add salt and pepper to taste.

Roast in the preheated oven for 1½ hours or until vegetables are tender and golden, basting every 20 minutes. When there is 10 minutes of cooking time left, add the drained and cooked beans to the vegetables and toss thoroughly to combine. Return to the oven for the final 10 minutes.

When the cooking time has finished, remove the baking dish from the oven and squeeze all the soft garlic pulp onto the vegetables. Toss well to combine then add the herbs and salt and freshly ground pepper to taste.

*You may use canned beans which should be rinsed before using or dried beans if you prefer. To use dried beans, soak 150g (5oz) in cold water for several hours then drain. Bring the beans to the boil in a pan of water and simmer until tender, about 1 hour then drain.

Fijian Kokoda

(photographed on page 101)

This light and fabulously flavoured fish salad is typical of the cooking of Fiji, where local produce is used at its peak to highlight local flavours. As the fish is cured rather than cooked, it is important that this salad is eaten on the day it is made. Although coconut milk is used here, it only serves to marinate the fish and is mostly discarded, hence the incredibly low fat result.

Ingredients

1.5kg (3 ½ lb) firm white fish
1 cup fresh lime juice (or lemon juice)
300ml (10oz) canned coconut milk
salt and pepper to taste

1 small red capsicum, finely diced
1 small green capsicum, finely diced
1 small red chilli, minced
1 firm tomato, finely diced

lime or lemon wedges, for garnish

Method

Cut the fish into 1cm (½") cubes and mix with 200ml (7oz) of the lime juice, half the coconut milk, salt and pepper to taste. Stir well and marinate overnight or for at least 4 hours.

When the fish is firm and looks opaque (cooked), drain away and discard the liquid.

Mix the drained fish with the capsicum pieces, chilli and tomato. Add the remaining coconut milk and lime juice and stir to combine thoroughly.

Serve cold in glasses with wedges of lime or lemon as an entrée.

Asian Gingered Coleslaw

The fresh flavours in this summery salad are a perfect match for rich and textured fish such as grilled tuna or salmon. The salad can be made a day ahead, as can the dressing, but they should not be combined until you are almost ready to serve. The lovely low fat dressing adds incredible depth of flavour.

Serves 6

Ingredients

½ large curly cabbage, very finely sliced, about 5 cups
4 baby bok choy, leaves separated and sliced
8 spring onions, julienned lengthways
200g (7oz) can sliced water chestnuts, drained
2 medium carrots, finely julienned
2 stalks lemon grass, very finely sliced
4 kaffir lime leaves, very finely sliced

Dressing:
2 tablespoons low fat mayonnaise
2 tablespoons low fat yoghurt
juice of 2 lemons
juice of 1 lime
1 tablespoon freshly grated ginger
4 tablespoons rice vinegar
salt and pepper to taste

Garnish:
1 bunch of coriander, well washed and roughly chopped
½ cup toasted peanuts or sunflower seeds

Method

Finely slice the cabbage and mix in a large bowl with the sliced bok choy, julienne spring onions, water chestnuts, julienne carrots and finely sliced lemon grass and lime leaves. Toss thoroughly.

In a jug, whisk together all the dressing ingredients until smooth and well seasoned then pour over the salad ingredients and toss thoroughly until all the vegetables are coated with the dressing.

To serve, mix through the coriander at the last minute and sprinkle with the crushed peanuts or sunflower seeds.

Japanese Rice Noodle Salad

Cool rice noodles are a great way to add interest to a main course. They are quick and easy to make and most can be made a day ahead. Remember to follow the instructions here for soaking the noodles (disregard directions on the packet of rice noodles as the translations are often misleading).

Ingredients

250g (8oz) long, flat rice noodles

1 teaspoon olive oil
2 teaspoons freshly grated ginger
1-2 small fresh red chillies, seeded and minced
1 red capsicum, cut into small chunks
6 spring onions, sliced on the diagonal

½ bunch coriander

juice of 1 lime
1 tablespoon Japanese rice vinegar
1 tablespoon soy sauce
2 tablespoons vegetable stock
3 tablespoons sesame seeds

Method

Fill a large jug or bowl with hand-hot water and immerse the rice noodles, allowing them to soak until soft, about 5-10 minutes. Drain and rinse under cold water to refresh them, then place the noodles in a large mixing bowl.

Heat the olive oil in a small non-stick pan and add the ginger and chillies and sauté gently for a minute or two. Add the chopped capsicum pieces and raise the heat to medium high and stir fry the capsicum pieces until they are softened. Add the spring onion slices and continue to cook for a further 2 minutes.

Tip the capsicum mixture into the mixing bowl with the noodles and add the coriander, tossing thoroughly.

In a small jug, whisk together the lime juice, rice vinegar, soy and stock and toss through the noodles. Sprinkle with the sesame seeds and chill before serving.

Marinated Salmon, Cucumber and Daikon Salad

There is something slightly exotic and almost decadent about serving marinated salmon. In this simple recipe the salmon is first marinated before being sliced thinly and served with a light and easy salad.

Serves 6

Ingredients

700g (1½ lb) fillet of salmon, centre cut

6 tablespoons mirin (sweet Japanese rice wine)
3 tablespoons Japanese soy sauce
1 tablespoon fresh grated ginger
1 teaspoon toasted sesame oil

1 continental cucumber
1 teaspoon sea salt
1 tablespoon caster sugar
3 tablespoons rice vinegar

curly endive, well washed and dried
1 daikon (white radish), finely julienned

Method

Ask your fishmonger to slice the salmon thinly as for smoked salmon. If they can't or won't, have the skin removed and slice the salmon into very thin strips—if you feel you are able to slice the salmon on an angle this would be desirable, but if not, cut straight down.

Whisk the mirin, soy, ginger and sesame oil together then remove 2 tablespoons and reserve. Pour the remainder into a shallow bowl and add the sliced salmon fillet, allowing the fish to marinate for 2 hours.

Meanwhile, peel the cucumber and using a vegetable peeler or food slicer cut the cucumber into long, thin slices and place these in a bowl. Mix together the sea salt, sugar and rice vinegar and drizzle over the cucumber, tossing well to coat the slices in the dressing.

Arrange slices of marinated salmon on the plates then place the curly endive and white radish in the centre. Weave some drained cucumber slices through the salad then drizzle a little of the reserved mirin dressing over the salad.

Oven-roasted Tomato and Eggplant Fans with Summer Herbs

When being inventive and still trying to follow a low fat diet, you'll find roasting at high temperatures a real plus. The extreme heat of the oven locks in the flavour, requiring almost no fat to add richness. This appetizer is so delicious and very easy to make.

Serves 6

Ingredients

3 small eggplants

4-5 Roma tomatoes
2 cloves garlic, minced
1 tablespoon olive oil
10 basil leaves
2 tablespoons fresh rosemary

60g (2oz) feta cheese, crumbled
salt and cracked black pepper to taste

extra basil sprigs

Method

Preheat the oven to 250°C (475°F).

Halve the eggplants lengthways then, with the cut surface resting on a board, cut the eggplant into $\frac{1}{2}$ cm ($\frac{1}{4}$") slices, beginning the cuts about 2cm ($\frac{3}{4}$") from the core end. Turn the eggplant fans over and sprinkle with salt. Allow to rest for 30 minutes then rinse and dry thoroughly.

Meanwhile, slice the tomatoes lengthways. Mix the minced garlic with the olive oil and set aside.

When the eggplant fans have been washed and dried, place them on non-stick oven trays and place a slice of tomato in between every 2 slices of eggplant so that you have alternating eggplant and tomato slices. Tear the basil leaves and insert between the tomato and eggplant slices.

Brush the garlic oil over the eggplant and sprinkle with finely chopped rosemary.

Bake the eggplant fans at 250°C (475°F) for 15 minutes then remove from the oven. Crumble the feta cheese over the eggplant fans then add salt and cracked black pepper to taste. Return to the oven for a further 5 minutes or until the cheese browns slightly.

Garnish with extra basil sprigs and black pepper, drizzle with extra olive oil and serve immediately.

Tuna Barley Niçoise

The traditional French salad Niçoise has always been a dieters delight. It is high in nutrients, low in fat and full of flavour. This is my modern variation on an already well-established theme but adds more texture and interest. Don't let the long ingredient list deter you, this salad is quick and easy to make!   **Serves 6**

Ingredients

Salad: 2 pink potatoes, unpeeled
1 teaspoon olive oil or olive oil spray
sea salt and pepper
2 teaspoons fresh rosemary
1 litre (33oz) mild vegetable stock
1 teaspoon fresh oregano (or ½ dried)
1 teaspoon fresh marjoram (or ½ dried)
1 cup pearl barley
1 Spanish onion, finely sliced
6 tuna steaks (about 180g/6½ oz each)

500g (1lb) green beans, blanched
½ cup chopped fresh parsley

handful of baby lettuce leaves (mesclun)
2 hard boiled eggs, sliced
2 red capsicums, roasted

Dressing: juice of 3 lemons
juice of 1 lime
1 tablespoon red wine vinegar

2 tablespoons anchovy paste
4 cloves garlic, minced
1 teaspoon mixed dried herbs
1-2 tablespoons virgin olive oil
1 teaspoon Dijon mustard
½ cup vegetable stock

Garnish: 2 Roma tomatoes,
finely chopped
150g (5oz) kalamata olives, finely chopped

Method

Wash the potatoes well and slice (do not peel). Brush lightly (or spray) with olive oil. Sprinkle with sea salt, pepper and rosemary and bake on oven trays at 220°C (430°F) for 45 minutes, turning during the cooking time.

Bring the stock to a boil and add the oregano and marjoram. Add the barley, cover and simmer for 40 minutes. Remove from heat and set aside. Soak the finely sliced Spanish onion in cold water for 30 minutes, then drain.

Season the tuna steaks with salt and pepper and cook on a preheated grill pan for 2 minutes each side, until just cooked, or alternatively bake at 210°C (420°F) for 7 minutes.

To make the dressing, whisk together all ingredients until thick then set aside. Mix green beans, onions rings, parsley and half the dressing with the warm barley and toss thoroughly to distribute.

To assemble, place several slices of potato on the centre of each plate, top with 3 or 4 lettuce leaves, a generous spoonful of barley mixture, some egg slices, some roasted capsicum and a cooked fillet of tuna. Place teaspoonfuls of finely chopped tomato and olives around the salad, then drizzle everything with remaining dressing. Sprinkle with remaining parsley and serve at room temperature.

Tuscan Tomato and Bean Salad

This hearty yet refreshing salad can be made well ahead of time and is a perfect accompaniment to a rich and satisfying pasta. Watercress and rocket (rucola in Italian) add a peppery finish to the sweet flavour of summer tomato.

Ingredients

1 cup boiling water
12 sundried tomatoes, drained

$\frac{1}{3}$ cup rice vinegar
1 tablespoon olive oil
2 teaspoons molasses
1 tablespoon soy sauce
salt and pepper (optional)

150g (5oz) baby rocket leaves
150g (5oz) watercress
8 Roma tomatoes, diced
6 spring onions, sliced
80g (3oz) kalamata olives, stones removed
2 x 440g (2 x 15½ oz) cans cannellini beans, rinsed and drained

100g (3½ oz) chopped toasted walnuts

Method

Combine the boiling water and drained sundried tomatoes and allow to stand until the water cools. Add the rice vinegar, oil, molasses and soy sauce and purée in a food processor until smooth. Add salt and pepper if desired.

Thoroughly wash the rocket and watercress until no trace of grit remains. Place the freshly washed leaves in a large mixing bowl and add the diced tomatoes, spring onions, olives and cannellini beans.

Pour over the sundried tomato dressing and toss well to coat all the leaves. Serve immediately garnished with the toasted walnuts.

Vietnamese Herbed Rice Noodles with Peanuts and Asparagus

This Vietnamese-inspired side dish is light, fresh and full of flavour and makes a perfect accompaniment for any fish such as tuna or salmon. It keeps very well for a day or two so you can make it a day ahead if necessary.

Ingredients

3 tablespoons rice vinegar
1 tablespoon sugar
1 small Spanish onion, finely sliced

250g (8oz) dried rice noodles

2 bunches of asparagus

$\frac{1}{3}$ cup chopped fresh mint
$\frac{1}{3}$ cup chopped fresh coriander
1 continental cucumber, peeled, seeded and thinly sliced
6 spring onions, finely sliced
3 Roma tomatoes, finely diced
$\frac{3}{4}$ cup roasted peanuts, lightly crushed

juice of 2 limes
2 teaspoons fish sauce
2 teaspoons olive oil
$\frac{1}{2}$ teaspoon chilli flakes

Method

First, whisk the rice vinegar and sugar together and pour over the finely sliced onion rings. Allow to marinate for 1 hour, tossing frequently.

Cook noodles according to packet directions (usually, rice noodles need only to soak in boiling water for 5 minutes, otherwise, boil for 1-2 minutes then drain immediately and rinse under cold water).

Cut off the tough stalk of the asparagus, and cut the remaining stalks into 2cm (¾") lengths. Simmer the asparagus in salted water for 2 minutes until bright green and crisp-tender. Rinse in cold water to refresh.

Toss the noodles with the reserved onion/vinegar mixture while still warm, then using kitchen scissors, cut the noodles into manageable lengths.

To the noodles, add the cooked asparagus, chopped mint, coriander, cucumber, spring onions, tomatoes and roasted peanuts and toss thoroughly.

Whisk the lime juice, fish sauce, oil and chilli flakes together and drizzle over the noodle salad.

Serve at room temperature.

Salad Dressings with New Flavours

*C*reating your own fabulous salad combinations is very rewarding, but sometimes you need a little bit of inspiration to create the perfect dressing.

*E*veryone has different ideas about the texture and thickness of a salad dressing. Some people like thick, creamy dressings that coat the salad ingredients generously while others prefer a light and acidic dressing which just flavours the salad in a subtle way.

*W*hatever your preference, you will find some innovative new flavour combinations here which will help you to create your own perfect salad.

Light and Acidic Salad Dressings

Roasted Garlic Vinaigrette

Makes approx. ¾ cup

1 large head garlic
1 tablespoon olive oil
3 tablespoons boiling water
3 tablespoons balsamic vinegar
2 teaspoons extra virgin olive oil
1 teaspoon Dijon mustard
salt and cracked pepper to taste

Separate the garlic cloves but do not peel. Toss them with the olive oil and place in a small ovenproof baking dish. Bake at 220°C (430°F) for 20-30 minutes until the cloves are golden brown. Remove from the oven and cool.

When the cloves are cool enough to handle, thoroughly squeeze the soft roasted garlic out of each clove, discarding the skins. Purée the garlic with the boiling water, balsamic vinegar, extra virgin olive oil and mustard, adding salt and pepper to taste.

Goes well with: • Potato salads
• Salad of green beans with toasted nuts
• Fresh tuna or salmon

Chinese Ginger Hoisin Vinaigrette

Makes approx. 1 cup

3 tablespoons hoisin sauce (Chinese barbecue sauce)
3 tablespoons white wine vinegar
3 tablespoons chicken stock
1 tablespoon peanut oil
1 tablespoon toasted sesame oil
1 tablespoon minced or grated fresh ginger
1 tablespoon soy sauce
2 teaspoons mustard of your choice

Purée all ingredients in a food processor until smooth then add salt to taste if desired. Use immediately or store in the refrigerator for up to 1 week. Allow to come back to room temperature then whisk thoroughly before using.

Goes well with: • Blanched asparagus
• Asian noodle salads
• Salads with thinly sliced beef and Asian vegetables and herbs

Warm Shallot and Lemon Dressing

Makes approx. ¾ cup

4 large golden shallots
2 cloves garlic (optional)
3 tablespoons vegetable oil
juice of 2 fresh lemons
grated zest of 1 lemon
3 tablespoons vegetable stock
salt and pepper to taste

Peel and mince the shallots and garlic.

Heat the oil in a small frypan until smoking then add the chopped shallots and garlic and sauté until translucent, about 5 minutes.

Whisk in the lemon juice, lemon zest and vegetable stock. Add salt and pepper to taste and simmer briefly. Remove from the heat and allow to cool slightly before using.

Goes well with: • Baby spinach or rocket
• Fresh tomatoes, sliced or quartered
• Cold poached chicken or other poultry

Vietnamese Lime, Chilli and Herb Dressing

Makes 1 cup

4 tablespoons Asian fish sauce
4 tablespoons fresh lime juice
3 tablespoons water
2 tablespoons palm sugar
1-2 small hot red chillies
6 cloves garlic
20g (⅔ oz) piece fresh ginger, peeled

Whisk together the fish sauce, lime juice, water and palm sugar until the sugar has dissolved. Finely mince the chillies with the garlic cloves and ginger then whisk in the liquid. Allow the flavours to blend for 5 minutes then toss with your salad.

Goes well with: • All types of Asian noodles
• Warm salads with thinly sliced beef, water chestnuts, etc.
• Salads of shellfish mixed with Asian greens

Japanese Ginger Miso Vinaigrette

Makes 1 cup

4 tablespoons rice vinegar
1 tablespoon miso*
2 teaspoons minced fresh ginger
1 large garlic clove, minced
2 tablespoons toasted sesame seeds
6 fresh basil leaves, finely sliced
1/4 teaspoon dried red chilli flakes
100ml (3 1/2 oz) peanut oil
     *Soy bean paste—available from Asian food stores

Whisk together the rice vinegar, miso, minced ginger, minced garlic, toasted sesame seeds and basil with the chilli flakes then slowly whisk in the oil a little at a time until it has all been added.

Goes well with: • Oven-roasted eggplant
              • Hokkien noodles
              • Asian stir-fried vegetables

Fresh Parsley Vinaigrette

Makes 1 1/2 cups

1 bunch fresh Italian parsley
6 tablespoons red wine vinegar
2 cloves garlic, optional
1 cup olive oil

Wash and dry the parsley. Place the parsley in a food processor with the vinegar and garlic and process until the parsley is well chopped.

   With the mixer running, add the olive oil in a thin stream and continue processing until the dressing is thick. Season with salt and pepper to taste and use at room temperature.

Goes well with: • Roasted Italian vegetables
              • Baby rocket leaves with croutons and Parmesan shavings
              • Salads of summer tomatoes, basil, olives

Thicker, Richer Salad Dressings

Indonesian Satay Sauce

Makes about 1 cup

2 tablespoons peanut oil
5 cloves garlic, minced
½ small red chilli minced
5 tablespoons peanut butter
1½ tablespoons tomato paste
3 tablespoons hoisin sauce (Chinese barbecue sauce)
1 teaspoon sugar
1 teaspoon fish sauce
¾ cup water
¼ cup peanuts, crushed

Heat the oil and sauté the garlic and minced chilli until softened, about 2 minutes, then add all remaining ingredients and whisk while heating. Bring to the boil and simmer until thickened slightly, about 3 minutes.

Suggested uses: • Cold sliced chicken or lamb
• Crisp noodles with crunchy Asian vegetables, like bok choy

Turkish Hazelnut and Garlic Dressing

Makes about a cup

2 slices peasant-style white bread, crusts removed
180g (6½ oz) toasted hazelnuts
3 cloves garlic, minced
zest and juice of a lemon
1 tablespoon white wine vinegar
½ cup olive oil
3 tablespoons plain yoghurt
sea salt to taste

Toast the bread until golden then tear into small pieces and place in a food processor and process until crumbs form. Add the hazelnuts, garlic and lemon zest and process until the nuts are well crushed then, with the motor running, add the lemon juice, vinegar and olive oil.

Finally, add the yoghurt and process briefly. Season to taste then set aside.

Goes well with: • Shellfish and cold poached salmon
• Boiled cool potatoes
• Blanched green beans and crisp vegetables

Real Homemade Herb Mayonnaise

Makes about ¹/₂ cup

300ml (10oz) olive oil
300ml (10oz) grapeseed oil
2 cups fresh herbs of your choice—parsley, chives, basil, chervil, etc.
2 cloves garlic, peeled
2 eggs
2 egg yolks
¹/₂-1 tablespoon French Dijon mustard
1 tablespoon white wine vinegar
salt and pepper to taste

Combine the olive and grapeseed oils and set aside. Process the herbs and garlic until chopped and set aside.

Place the eggs and egg yolks in a food processor and process for 2 minutes. While processing, add the mustard and half the vinegar and then add the oil mixture in a thin stream. When most of the oil has been used, stop the processor and add the herb mixture, remaining vinegar and remaining oil and process briefly to combine. Add salt and pepper to taste and chill until ready to use. Store in the refrigerator.

Goes well with: • Everything!

Coriander Chilli 'Mayonnaise'

Makes about ¹/₂ cup

1 small red fresh chilli
1 large bunch fresh coriander
3 tablespoons sour cream
3 tablespoons plain yoghurt
2 garlic cloves, chopped
6 mint leaves
juice and zest of 1 lime
salt and pepper to taste

Remove and discard the seeds of the chilli and wash and dry the coriander.

Place the sour cream, yoghurt, garlic, mint leaves, chilli and coriander leaves in a food processor and process until smooth. Add the lime juice and zest and process briefly, then add salt and pepper to taste.

Goes well with: • Flaked cold salmon
• Warm boiled baby potatoes
• Avocado and asparagus

Weights and Measures

Dry Measures

All the measures are level, so when you have filled a cup or spoon, level it off with the edge of a knife. The exact conversions are: 1oz = 28g and 100g = 3½oz.

Note that the "cook's equivalent" of 1kg is 2lb.

METRIC	IMPERIAL		METRIC	IMPERIAL	
15g	½oz		255g	9oz	
20g	⅔oz		280g	10oz	
30g	1oz		310g	11oz	
60g	2oz		340g	12oz	¾lb
90g	3oz		370g	13oz	
125g	4oz	¼lb	400g	14oz	
145g	5oz		425g	15oz	
170g	6oz		455g	16oz	1lb
200g	7oz		1000g 1kg	35oz	2lb 3oz
230g	8oz	½lb	1.5kg	53oz	3lb 5oz

g = grams **oz** = ounces **kg** = kilograms **lb** = pound

Length

These conversions are only approximate. To convert inches to centimetres, multiply inches by 2.54. Therefore, 1" = 2.54cm and 1cm = 0.3937".

METRIC	IMPERIAL	METRIC	IMPERIAL
0.5cm	¼"	15cm	6"
1.0cm	½"	18cm	7"
2.0cm	¾"	20cm	8"
2.5cm	1"	23cm	9"
5cm	2"	25cm	10"
8cm	3"	28cm	11"
10cm	4"	30cm	1', 12"
12cm	5"		

mm = millimetres **cm** = centimetres **"** = inches **'** = feet

Oven Temperatures

The temperatures given here are not exact; they have been rounded off and are given as a guide only. To convert °C to °F multiply °C by 9 and divide by 5, then add 32.

	°C	°F	Gas Mark
Very slow	120	250	1
Slow	150	300	2
Moderately slow	160	320	3
Moderate	180	350	4
Moderately hot	190-200	370-390	5-6
Hot	210-220	410-430	6-7
Very hot	230	450	8
Super hot	250-290	480-550	9-10

Liquid Measures

METRIC ml	IMPERIAL fl oz	CUP & SPOON
5ml	⅙ fl oz	1 teaspoon
20ml	⅔ fl oz	1 tablespoon
30ml	1 fl oz	1 tablespoon plus 2 teaspoons
60ml	2 fl oz	¼ cup
85ml	2¾ fl oz	⅓ cup
100ml	3½ fl oz	⅜ cup
125ml	4 fl oz	½ cup
150ml	5 fl oz	⅔ cup
250ml	8½ fl oz	1 cup
300ml	10 fl oz	1⅕ cup
360ml	12 fl oz	1½ cups
420ml	14 fl oz	1¾ cups
500ml	16½ fl oz	2 cups
600ml	20 fl oz	2½ cups
1 litre	33 fl oz	4 cups

Glossary

antipasto: an assortment of cold meats, vegetables and cheeses, often marinated, served as an hors d'oeurve

beetroot: regular round beet

beurre bosc pears: variety of pear with slender neck and yellow-brown skin

cannellini: white kidney beans

capsicum: bell pepper

chickpeas: garbanzos

chillies: chilli peppers

coriander: cilantro

cumquat: oblong fruit with sour pulp but a sweet rind, also spelt kumquat

daikon: giant, white radish, Japanese

Desiree potatoes: winter potato with red skin, yellow flesh and oval shape, good for boiling and baking

entrée: in Australia and Europe, the "entry" or hors d'oeuvre, and is the meaning used in this book; in the US entrée means the main course

feta: a salty, Greek-style white cheese made from ewes' milk

ghee: clarified butter—the clear, yellow liquid remaining when butter is gently heated and allowed to cool, and the proteins come out of solution and fall to the bottom

Hokkien noodles: Chinese egg noodles

jam: jelly in the US

jîcama: large, bulbous root vegetable with a sweet, nutty flavour, also called Mexican potato

julienne: vegetables cut into thin strips

kaffir lime leaves: glossy, dark green leaves with a citrus aroma

kalamata: dark, Greek olive marinated in olive oil or vinegar

kecap manis: syrupy-thick Indonesian soy sauce, sweetened with palm sugar and seasoned with garlic and star anise

minced: ground into very small pieces

mirin: Japanese sweet, syrupy rice wine for cooking

nigella seeds: also called black onion seeds; they have a nutty, peppery flavour

orzo: tiny, rice-shaped pasta

panzanella: Italian salad containing bread

prawn: shrimp

punnet: small basket, approx. 8 oz

rocket (arugula): a peppery, piquant lettuce

Roma tomatoes: sauce tomatoes

sambal oelek: a condiment consisting of chillies, brown sugar and salt

sauté: to cook or brown in a small amount of hot fat

shallots: French eschallots

soba noodles: Japanese noodles made from buckwheat and wheat flour

Spanish onion: purple onion

Splenda®: artificial sweetener containing maltodextrin and sucralose, as sweet as sugar by weight

spring onions: scallions

sugar snaps: snap peas with edible pods

sundried tomatoes: dried tomatoes

tatsoi leaves: spoon-shaped leaves of a mild oriental mustard plant

zest (lemon, etc.): thin outer layer of citrus fruits containing the aromatic citrus oil; it is usually thinly pared with a vegetable peeler, or grated with a zester or grater to separate it from the bitter white pith underneath